CONTENTS

KU-713-009

INTRODUCTION

The story of the Israelites and how they came to live in the Promised Land

The stories of the Old Testament give a vivid account of the fortunes of one people, the Israelites or Hebrews.

From the story of Adam and Eve through those of Joseph and of Samson, to the return to Jerusalem after years of exile, this book brings the great events of Bible times to life. It tells how Abraham received a promise from God that his descendants would form one nation. God said that, as long as they obeyed his laws, he would lead the Israelites to the Promised Land.

So we learn how, from their beginnings as wandering nomads, the Israelites grew to become a powerful nation with a small empire under their kings David and Solomon, only then to lose it all and be sent into exile.

But what do we know about everyday life in Bible times? This book draws on historical evidence to show how people lived and went about their daily tasks; how they built in times of peace and how they fought in times of war. It shows what they wore and the objects they used every day; how they travelled and how they worked the land. The people and times of the Bible come to life through the illustrations and maps that accompany the stories retold here.

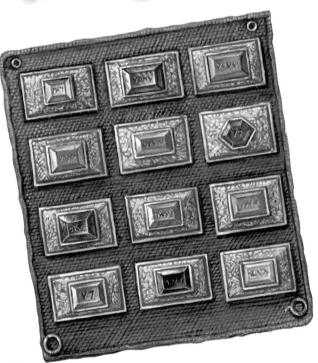

An Israelite high priest at the time of Solomon would have worn a breast plate (left) inlaid with precious stones. Every stone was inscribed with the name of the ancestor of each of the twelve tribes of Israel.

The people of the Bible lived in the area surrounded by the rectangle (right). All the historical maps in this book are located within this outlined area.

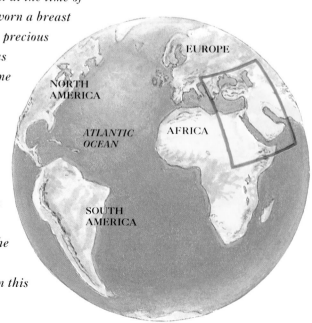

EUROPE

NORTH AMERICA

ATLANTIC OCEAN

AFRICA

SOUTH AMERICA

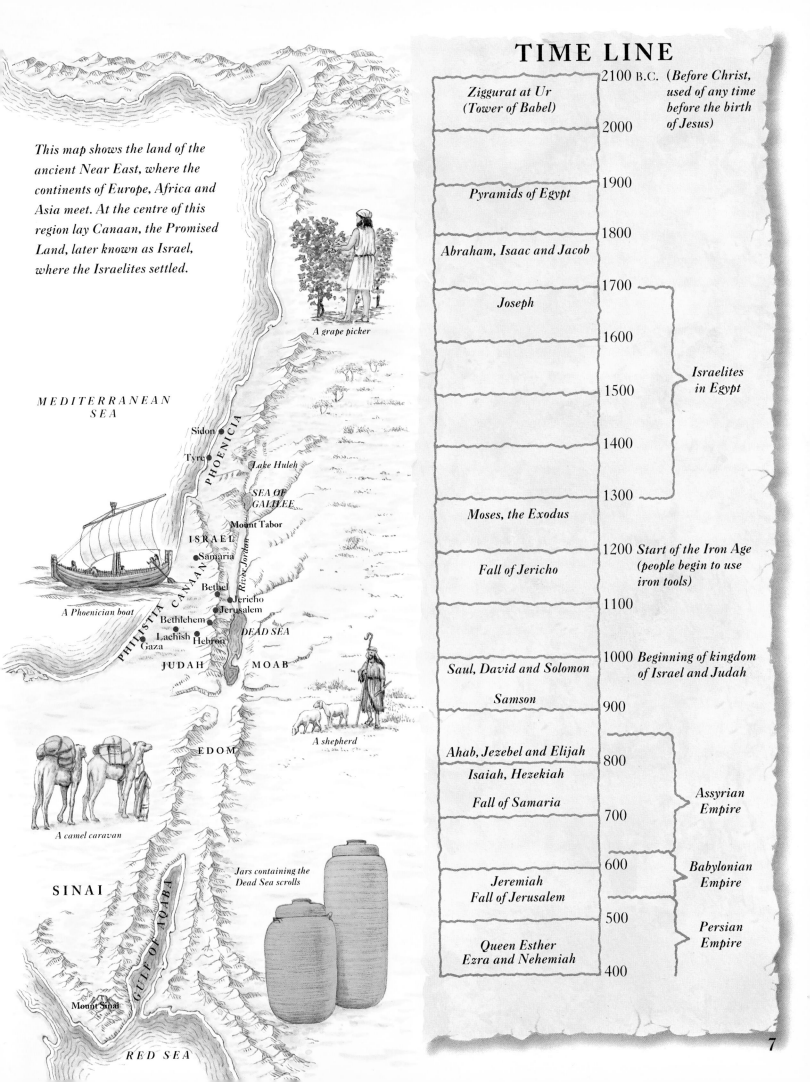

This map shows the land of the ancient Near East, where the continents of Europe, Africa and Asia meet. At the centre of this region lay Canaan, the Promised Land, later known as Israel, where the Israelites settled.

A grape picker

MEDITERRANEAN SEA

Sidon

PHOENICIA

Tyre

Lake Huleh

SEA OF GALILEE

Mount Tabor

ISRAEL

Samaria

CANAAN

Bethel

River Jordan

Jericho

Jerusalem

A Phoenician boat

PHILISTIA

Bethlehem

Lachish

Hebron

DEAD SEA

Gaza

JUDAH

MOAB

EDOM

A shepherd

A camel caravan

SINAI

GULF OF AQABA

Jars containing the Dead Sea scrolls

Mount Sinai

RED SEA

TIME LINE

Ziggurat at Ur (Tower of Babel)	2100 B.C. *(Before Christ, used of any time before the birth of Jesus)*
	2000
Pyramids of Egypt	1900
	1800
Abraham, Isaac and Jacob	
	1700
Joseph	1600
	1500 *Israelites in Egypt*
	1400
	1300
Moses, the Exodus	
	1200 *Start of the Iron Age (people begin to use iron tools)*
Fall of Jericho	1100
Saul, David and Solomon	1000 *Beginning of kingdom of Israel and Judah*
Samson	900
Ahab, Jezebel and Elijah	800
Isaiah, Hezekiah	
Fall of Samaria	700 *Assyrian Empire*
	600 *Babylonian Empire*
Jeremiah Fall of Jerusalem	500 *Persian Empire*
Queen Esther Ezra and Nehemiah	400

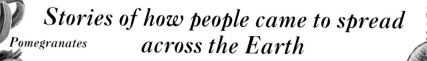

THE FIRST PEOPLE

Stories of how people came to spread across the Earth

Pomegranates

Figs

Adam and Eve

God created Heaven and Earth and all kinds of animals to fill the world. The moon and the stars shone in the sky and gave light at night. The sun gave light during the day. But there was nobody to look after God's creation, so God made a man out of the dust and breathed life into his nostrils. God called the man Adam.

God planted a garden in the eastern part of Eden, with a river flowing through it that divided into four streams. God put fruit, trees and plants in Eden for Adam to eat and enjoy. The Garden of Eden was so beautiful that it has been called paradise—a place people think is like Heaven. God gave the garden to Adam to look after. But in the middle of the garden God planted two trees: the tree of life and the tree of the knowledge of good and evil. Adam was not supposed to eat the fruit of these trees.

God brought all kinds of animals to Eden but none was a suitable companion for Adam. When Adam was asleep, God took one of his ribs and made a woman out of it.

The snake knew about the fruit from the trees in the middle of Eden. The

A turtle dove

Four rivers flowed through the Garden of Eden: the Pishon, the Gihon, the Tigris and the Euphrates. These rivers made the land very fertile so that many different plants and animals thrived there. The Tigris and the Euphrates rivers still exist today but, because the Pishon and the Gihon have disappeared, we do not know where the Garden of Eden was—although it was probably in Mesopotamia, an area now covered by the country of Iraq.

The fruit of the tree of knowledge is often thought to have been an apple, but it is much more likely that the fruit would have been a pomegranate, since they are more common in this area than apples.

Olives

An early picture of Adam and Eve and the tree of life from a Mesopotamian cylinder seal.

When evening came, Adam and the woman heard God in the garden. They suddenly felt embarrassed because they were naked and hid in the trees. But God called for them, so they told him what had happened.

God was furious. The snake, the man and the woman were all punished for disobeying God. From that time on the snake would crawl on its belly, the woman would give birth to children in great pain and the man would have to work hard on the land all his life.

Adam named the woman Eve. God still loved the first people and gave them clothes before he sent them out of the Garden of Eden into the world.

woman told the snake that if she ate the fruit she would die. The snake said, 'Of course you will not die! God knows that if you eat the fruit, you will know the difference between good and evil.' The woman plucked the fruit from the tree, ate some of it and gave it to Adam.

Cain and Abel

Adam and Eve had many sons and daughters. Their first son was named Cain and he became a farmer, like his father. Later, a second son was born, named Abel, who became a shepherd.

The first people believed that everything was created by God and that some of what he provided should be returned to him. So to thank God for the vegetables that had grown, Cain built an altar out of stones and put the best crops on the top to offer to God. Abel also built a stone altar, but he took a young lamb and put it on the altar.

Shepherds and farmers believed God owned the soil and all that grew in it. It was their duty to offer back to God some of what he had let them grow.

God was pleased with the lamb that Abel had given as an offering. But he was not as pleased with Cain's offering. Cain was angry that God should prefer his brother's offering when he had worked so hard to grow his vegetables.

Cain was not only angry but also very jealous of his brother. 'Let's go out to the field,' he said to Abel one day, pretending to be friendly. While they were out in the field Cain could not control his anger any longer, and he attacked and killed his brother. Cain's anger turned to fear as he heard God call, 'Where is your brother Abel?' 'I don't know,' replied Cain in a panic, 'Am I

In biblical times, many people lived by farming the land. Farmers used simple tools such as ploughs to help them. A plough was made of wood and (later) iron and was used to break up the soil and mix the seeds into the earth. It would have been pulled by oxen or donkeys and steered by the farmer.

my brother's keeper?' 'What have you done?' God asked. But he knew exactly what had happened.

As Abel's blood seeped into the ground, Cain realized his terrible crime and held his head in despair. 'When you work the ground,' God told him, 'it will no longer give you crops. You will be a restless wanderer on the Earth.'

Cain could no longer be a farmer, the only work he knew, and he was afraid that anyone who recognized him would try to kill him. But God protected Cain by putting a mark on him. Anyone who found him would know that God protected him and would not try to seek revenge

Cain's descendants became metalworkers. This coppersmith is making a pattern on the side of a copper pot using a special tool. He would have made frying pans and pots, as well as weapons.

A shepherd looked after his flock, protecting it from attack by wild animals such as wolves. The flock would have included goats as well as sheep. The sheep were kept to supply people with wool and meat. The goats provided milk, hair and skins.

for the jealous murder of his brother Abel.

Cain became the founder of the Kenite clan, people who wandered through the deserts of Arabia on donkeys. They made tools out of iron and copper and musical instruments such as flutes and harps.

These travelling metalworkers were recognized by a metal badge worn on their foreheads. This badge may have been the 'mark' that God gave to Cain. It told other people that they were craftsmen and not rulers of the land. The name Cain means smith or metalworker.

The Kenite people later settled in the land which God gave to Moses and the Israelites, known as the Promised Land. They became neighbours and sometimes rivals of the Israelites.

Noah's Ark

One of the many thousands of descendants of Adam was Noah. He was a good man who lived in an evil time. When God saw how wicked his world had become, he decided to flood the Earth and destroy it all. He would spare only Noah and his family.

God told Noah to build an ark, in which only his family and the animals God provided would be safe from the flood. Noah and his three sons, Shem, Ham and Japheth, set about building the boat.

When the ark was ready, Noah took one pair, male and female, of every animal, and seven extra pairs of animals such as lambs to provide food for his family. Then the first drops of rain began to fall. They kept falling for forty days and forty nights and the ark floated on the water.

After the rain, when the water level had begun to drop again, a jolt at the bottom of the ark told Noah there was land beneath them. But only the tops of mountains were showing above the water. Noah sent out a raven, thinking that if it did not return, it would have found somewhere to settle. But the raven came back to the ark. After a

The ark was built from 'gopher wood', which comes from cypress trees and is like pine.

BUILDING A BOAT

The units of measurement used in this time included the cubit and the span. A cubit was the length of a man's arm from the elbow to the tip of his longest finger. A span was the width of his hand.

A span

A cubit

To cut planks of wood two men used a giant saw in a saw-pit. The man in the pit pushed the saw up through the trunk and the other man pushed it down.

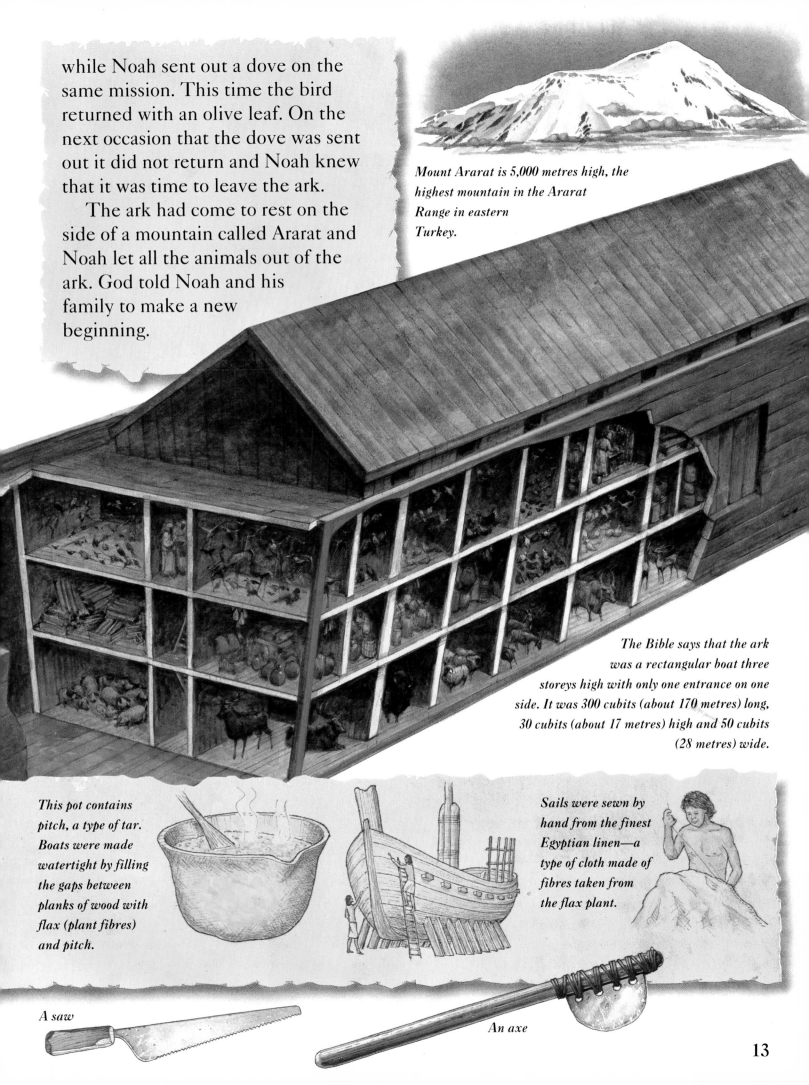

while Noah sent out a dove on the same mission. This time the bird returned with an olive leaf. On the next occasion that the dove was sent out it did not return and Noah knew that it was time to leave the ark.

The ark had come to rest on the side of a mountain called Ararat and Noah let all the animals out of the ark. God told Noah and his family to make a new beginning.

Mount Ararat is 5,000 metres high, the highest mountain in the Ararat Range in eastern Turkey.

The Bible says that the ark was a rectangular boat three storeys high with only one entrance on one side. It was 300 cubits (about 170 metres) long, 30 cubits (about 17 metres) high and 50 cubits (28 metres) wide.

This pot contains pitch, a type of tar. Boats were made watertight by filling the gaps between planks of wood with flax (plant fibres) and pitch.

Sails were sewn by hand from the finest Egyptian linen—a type of cloth made of fibres taken from the flax plant.

A saw

An axe

13

The Tower of Babel

After the flood, people sadly wandered the world in search of a land they could call their own. They finally came to Babylon on the River Euphrates. Here they decided to build a city with a tall tower that would reach up into the sky. They wanted to create something to be proud of.

They formed teams of builders. Some people made the bricks and others made the tar to stick the bricks together. Others were carriers; there was no shortage of people to help.

God saw what was happening and was not happy. He knew that people were trying to reach Heaven by themselves. 'I will mix up their language and scatter them over the whole world,' God decided. He named the tower 'Babel', which means 'to confuse'.

Arguments broke out and people could not work together because they could no longer understand each other. They fought, stopped building the city and moved away to find new places to live. From then on people in different parts of the world spoke different languages.

EUROPE

AFRICA

Large towers like the one at Babylon were quite common in Mesopotamia. There were over thirty at this time (around 2000 B.C.). The towers were called ziggurats. The Mesopotamians built them in order to make contact with their gods and held religious festivals there.

The ziggurat at Ur (right) was dedicated to the moon god. The king and his priest would climb the high stairways up the sides of the ziggurat. At the top there would be a shrine where they made offerings to the god.

14

According to the Bible, Noah's three sons, Shem, Ham and Japheth, became the ancestors of all the people in the world. Shem was the first of the ancient peoples who lived in the Near East and are known as Semites. His descendants included Abraham and Moses.

The Egyptians and Africans came from Ham. Japheth's descendants migrated to Europe, Asia Minor, Central Asia and India.

This Egyptian wall painting shows a group of Semitic people visiting Egypt.

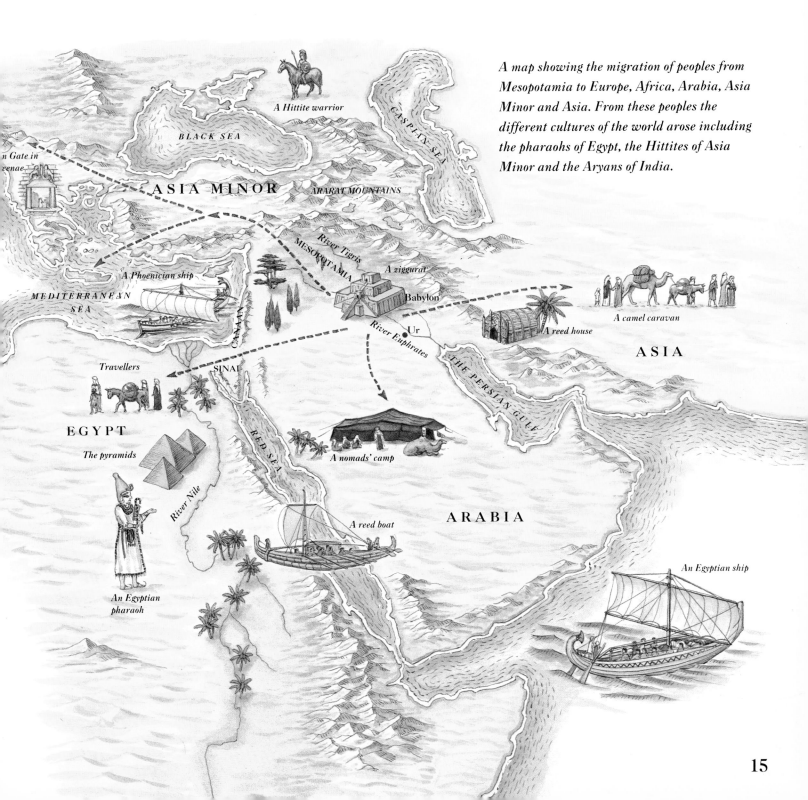

A map showing the migration of peoples from Mesopotamia to Europe, Africa, Arabia, Asia Minor and Asia. From these peoples the different cultures of the world arose including the pharaohs of Egypt, the Hittites of Asia Minor and the Aryans of India.

A Hittite warrior

BLACK SEA

CASPIAN SEA

n Gate in cenae

ASIA MINOR

ARARAT MOUNTAINS

River Tigris

MESOPOTAMIA

A ziggurat

Babylon

A Phoenician ship

MEDITERRANEAN SEA

CANAAN

River Euphrates

Ur

A reed house

ASIA

THE PERSIAN GULF

Travellers

SINAI

EGYPT

The pyramids

RED SEA

A nomads' camp

ARABIA

River Nile

An Egyptian ship

A reed boat

An Egyptian pharaoh

15

Stories of the first Israelites

Sodom and Gomorrah

Abraham, a descendant of Noah's son Shem, was the father of God's chosen people, the Israelites. One day Abraham's nephew, Lot, was sitting at the gateway to the city of Sodom when two angels arrived. Lot greeted them and invited them to dinner at his house. The angels accepted but were very cautious because they had heard that the men of the city were evil.

A crowd gathered outside Lot's house demanding to take away the angels. Lot tried to reason with them but the men said they would break down his door. Afraid of a riot, the angels pulled Lot inside and cast a spell of blindness on the violent mob.

The angels knew that it was only a matter of time before the mob broke into the house. 'Hurry!' they said to Lot. 'Get out of this place. God is about to destroy this wicked city.' Lot quickly passed the message on to his wife, his daughters and his sons-in-law.

When dawn was about to break, the

An earthquake may have caused the destruction of Sodom and Gomorrah. The cities were situated to the south of the Dead Sea and lay in fertile plains of lush green forests and vegetation. It is possible that great boulders of salt from the Dead Sea— which is very salty—fell into the cracks in the earth and were hurled up into the air when they met the heat in the cracks. Today, submerged forests lie at the southern end of the Dead Sea. It is thought that the whole area probably sank below sea level after an earthquake.

angels told Lot, 'Flee to the mountains, but whatever you do, don't look back.' Lot set off with his family, afraid of what would happen next.

When the sun had risen, Lot's family had travelled a fair distance out of the city. Strange weather suddenly came over the land. It seemed to be raining; but it was not water. Great balls of burning sulphur fell from the sky over the twin cities of Sodom and Gomorrah, which burst into flames. The air was thick with black smoke. Although Lot and his family were now a safe distance from the cities, Lot's wife forgot the angels' warning and looked back at the catastrophe. She was instantly turned into a pillar of salt.

The next morning the smoke was still rising in the air as Abraham came to comfort his nephew Lot who had lost his wife in the escape.

At the southern end of the Dead Sea, sticking out of the water, are pillars of salt that glisten as they catch the sun's rays. They look like floating statues. In the Bible story, Lot's wife turned into one of these pillars of salt.

17

The Promise to Abraham

When Abraham was seventy-five years old God told him to leave his home in Haran and go in search of another land. Abraham went south to Canaan with his wife Sarah, his nephew Lot, and all his possessions.

Times were hard: a famine forced Abraham to go to Egypt to find food. When he returned to Canaan, battles raged between rival kings.

One night Abraham lay worrying about his life: why had he left behind his livelihood and comfortable home? Life as a nomad was dangerous now, with neither a house nor land to farm.

Nomads like Abraham's family lived in tents. The tents were often made out of sheets of woven black goat hair almost two metres wide. The goat-hair cloth was draped across several poles and the ends were pegged into the ground like a modern-day tent.

Abraham was born in Ur in Mesopotamia. He then settled in Haran, farther north. On God's command he and his family travelled to Canaan. Later Abraham went to Egypt in search of food and then returned home to Canaan.

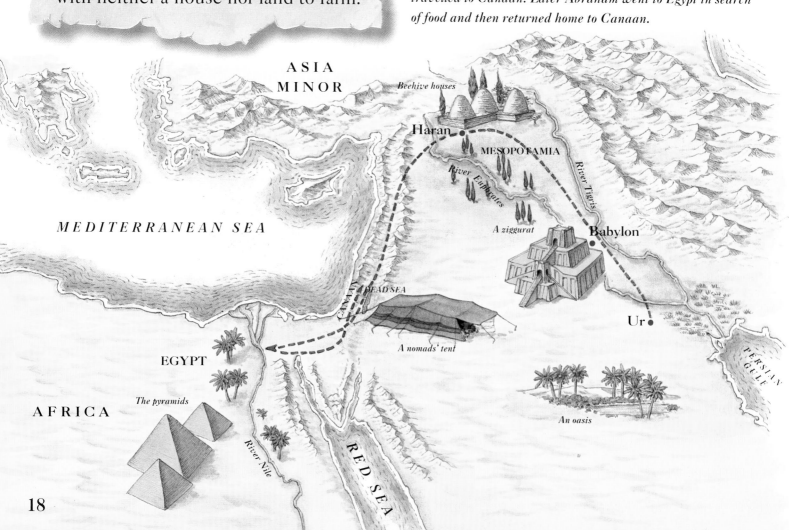

ASIA MINOR

Beehive houses

Haran

MESOPOTAMIA

River Euphrates

River Tigris

MEDITERRANEAN SEA

A ziggurat

Babylon

DEAD SEA

Ur

A nomads' tent

PERSIAN GULF

EGYPT

AFRICA

The pyramids

River Nile

RED SEA

An oasis

And he had no heir. Would his wife Sarah ever have a child?

Suddenly Abraham felt that God was there. 'Do not be afraid,' said a voice. 'Look up at the heavens and count the stars, if you can, for you will have as many descendants as there are stars.' As impossible as this seemed to Abraham, he believed it. He then fell asleep and dreamed that his descendants would be strangers in a foreign country and slaves for four hundred years. Then God said, 'I will give your descendants this land: from the River Nile in Egypt to the great River Euphrates.'

Because Sarah could not have children she told Abraham to have a child with Hagar, her maidservant. Hagar gave birth to a boy called Ishmael and Sarah felt sad knowing that she would never have a child.

One day three visitors came to Abraham and Sarah's tent. Abraham

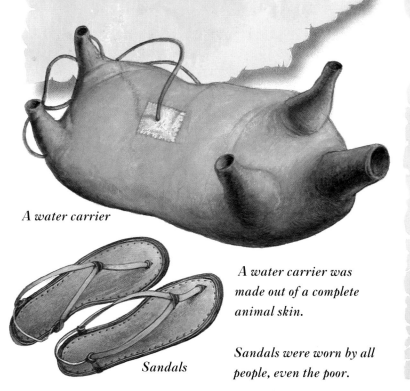

A water carrier

A water carrier was made out of a complete animal skin.

Sandals

Sandals were worn by all people, even the poor.

This small statue is of an Egyptian maidservant. The maid wears a wig and carries a basket on her head and a bird in her free hand. It was common for maids to wear wigs at this time. Egyptian maids like Hagar were in great demand.

and Sarah cooked them a meal. After dinner, the visitors predicted that, by the same time next year, Sarah would have a child. Sarah laughed at the prediction, though she secretly hoped it would come true.

Sure enough, before the year was out, Sarah gave birth to a son whom she named Isaac, which means 'laughter'. Abraham held a great feast to celebrate. During the feast, Ishmael started poking fun at his half-brother. When Sarah saw this she was furious and told Abraham to send Ishmael and his mother away.

With a sad heart Abraham sent them on their way with some food and water for their journey. This was soon used up and Hagar began to cry, for she knew her son was going to die. As she sat on the ground God spoke to her, 'Do not be afraid. I have heard the boy crying.' When Hagar opened her eyes, she saw a well and rushed over to it to get Ishmael water. God stayed with Ishmael as he grew up. He was the ancestor of the Ishmaelites, or Arab peoples.

Abraham and Isaac

God wanted to test Abraham's obedience, so he told him to take his son Isaac to the hills of Moriah and sacrifice him.

The next morning, with great sadness in his heart, Abraham took some wood and his donkey and set out. Abraham, Isaac and two servants travelled for three days before Abraham saw the hills of Moriah in the distance. The servants looked after the donkey while Abraham and Isaac went to pray. Isaac carried the wood, while Abraham carried the knife. Isaac asked his father where the lamb was that they were going to offer to God, but Abraham just replied that God would provide it.

When they reached the right place Abraham built a stone altar, arranged the wood on it, and then tied up his son on the altar. Abraham took the long knife and raised it above his head, ready to kill his son. He did not want to kill Isaac but Abraham knew he had to obey God. Just as God had given him Isaac, so God could take him away.

Abraham was about to plunge the knife into Isaac when a voice called, 'Abraham! Do not lay your hand on the boy. Do not do anything to him. For now I know that you are ready to sacrifice your own son for God.'

Abraham was overjoyed to hear God's command. Then he saw a ram caught in the branches of a small bush near by and sacrificed it as an offering to God.

AN ISRAELITE BURIAL
Bodies were washed, wrapped in cloth and buried quickly, usually within twenty-four hours of death.

The body was carried to burial by friends of the dead person.

ITEMS USED IN ANIMAL SACRIFICES

A knife

A rope

A stone figure of a Mesopotamian man carrying a sacrificial lamb. Abraham came from Ur in Mesopotamia.

Israelites of later generations worshipped in the hills of Moriah where Abraham's act of faith took place. Solomon built the first temple there, about a thousand years later (around 950 B.C.). The scene below shows the temple and the city of Jerusalem at the time of Solomon.

Only the wealthy could afford to buy land for tombs, such as the underground cave where Abraham's wife Sarah was buried.

An underground tomb

Stairs

Stone door

The first chamber

The burial chamber

An urn to hold the ashes of the animal.

Rams (left) and goats were sacrificed.

21

The Marriage of Isaac and Rebekah

Abraham lived to be a very old man and knew that he would soon die. Isaac, his son, now a grown man, was still unmarried. Abraham wanted Isaac to marry a woman from Haran, his old home in the north. So he instructed his servant to go to Haran in search of a woman from his ancient clan as a suitable wife for Isaac.

Abraham's servant selected ten of his master's camels for the journey and various precious gifts before setting off on his journey. He came to a town and made the camels kneel down by a well. It was nearly evening, the time when the women of the town came out to fetch water from the well. Abraham's servant prayed to God for a sign. He asked God to show him the woman he had chosen by having her give water to his camels without being asked.

A woman named Rebekah went down to the well to fill her jar with water. The servant asked her for a drink. She carefully drew water from the well and after she had given him a drink she gave water to his camels without his asking for it.

The servant took out a gold nose-ring and two gold bracelets and presented them to Rebekah. When he found out who Rebekah's father was, the servant was glad. He realized that he had found Abraham's relatives: Rebekah was the granddaughter of Abraham's brother,

The women of the family, including the older, unmarried girls, collected water every day from a well. The water was drawn from the well by dropping a leather bucket attached to a rope into the water. It was then pulled up by hand.

Nahor. The servant went with Rebekah to greet her family.

When Rebekah's father and her brother Laban heard the story, and all about Abraham's life since he had left Haran, they were overjoyed and agreed that Rebekah should marry Isaac. Abraham's servant brought out all his master's valuable gifts, and gave them to Rebekah's family, and they celebrated well into the night.

The next morning Abraham's servant and Rebekah and her maids set off on their camels to meet Isaac. They travelled a long way, and had nearly reached Abraham's home when Rebekah looked up from her camel and saw a man coming to meet them. She asked the servant who he was. 'He is my master, Isaac,' the servant replied. She covered herself with her veil and went to Isaac's camp to be married.

A wedding celebration. Every Israelite man had to marry— the marriage was usually arranged by parents when their children were still quite young. Sometimes the bride and groom were only eleven or twelve years old. It was quite common for cousins to marry.

Nose-rings were special tokens of marriage. Both men and women wore nose-rings, rings, bracelets and earrings. Most jewellery at this time was made out of gold, silver or bronze and was very simple in design.

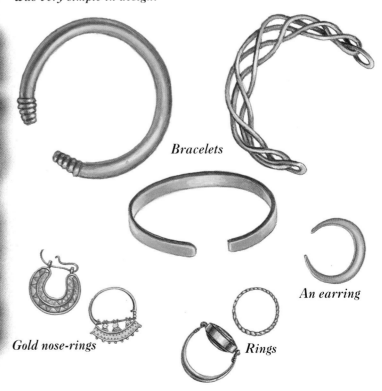

Bracelets

An earring

Gold nose-rings

Rings

Jacob and Esau

Isaac was forty when he married Rebekah. Soon after their marriage, Rebekah had twin boys. The first twin was named Esau, which means 'hairy', and the second was named Jacob, which means 'grasper of the heel' or 'cheat', because he came into the world hanging on to Esau.

Esau became a hunter who liked the outdoor life. Jacob was a quieter man who preferred to stay at home.

One day Esau came home from hunting to find Jacob cooking lentil

The Nubian ibex (below right) is a type of wild mountain goat that was hunted for its delicious meat. The Arabian oryx (below left) was also hunted.

stew. 'I'm starving,' he said to Jacob. 'Give me some of that red stew.' Jacob replied that Esau must sell him his inheritance before he could have the stew. 'I am about to die of starvation!' replied Esau. Then he thought, 'What is the use of this inheritance anyway; I want to eat now,' and he agreed to give his inheritance to Jacob for the stew.

Isaac was now an old, blind man. He called Esau, whom he loved more than Jacob, and asked him to go out and hunt some game animals for supper.

Jars like these were used to store flour, cooking oil, lentils and other foods and to keep them safe from blowing sand. The jars were also used to serve food at meal times.

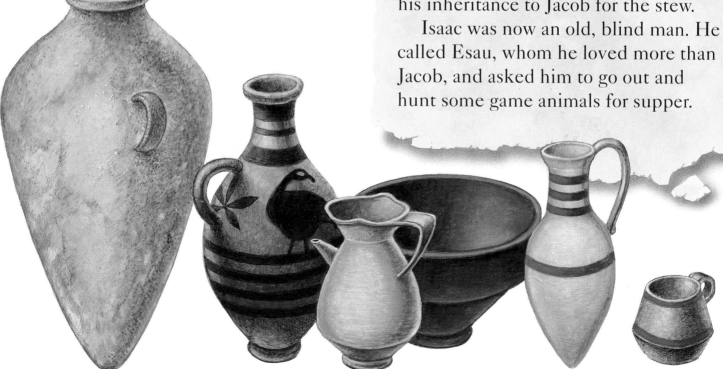

The fallow deer (left) would have been one of the animals hunted by Esau. The gazelle (below) represented grace and beauty to biblical peoples.

difference between his sons, but he still had his sense of touch. 'Come closer,' he said. He felt Jacob's hands and thought, the voice is Jacob's but the hands feel like Esau's.

After his meal Isaac said, 'Come here Esau.' When Isaac smelled his clothes, he was sure this was Esau and said, 'May God give you Heaven's dew and Earth's richness.'

No sooner had Isaac finished blessing Jacob than Esau returned and realized he had been tricked. He was furious and threatened to kill Jacob, saying 'That brother of mine has cheated me again!' But Isaac also gave Esau a blessing.

'Then I will bless you before I die,' Isaac told him. Isaac said that the son he blessed would rule over the other son. Esau went out to hunt. Rebekah overheard this conversation and planned to trick Isaac into giving Jacob his blessing.

Rebekah told Jacob to fetch two goats for her to cook in Isaac's favourite way. She then dressed Jacob in Esau's best clothes and covered his hands and neck with goatskins to make his skin feel as rough as Esau's.

When Rebekah had cooked the meal, Jacob nervously went into his father's tent and sat beside him. He said, 'I am Esau. I have done as you told me. Please sit up and eat some of my meat so that you may give me your blessing.' Isaac was suspicious and asked how he had hunted the animal so quickly. Jacob replied that God must have been with him this day. Isaac was too blind to see the

Israelite men and women wore a linen tunic underneath a wool tunic that reached from the neck to below the knees.

A girdle of leather or cloth was tied at the waist.

Rachel and Leah

Jacob escaped Esau's anger by travelling north to Abraham's old home of Haran to find a wife. After a long journey, Jacob stopped for the night. He dreamed of a stairway reaching up to heaven. At the top stood God who said, 'I am the God of Abraham, and the God of your father Isaac. I will give you and your descendants the land on which you are lying.' When Jacob woke up he built a pillar of stone and anointed it with oil to show that this was a special place. He named the place Bethel, or 'House of God'.

Jacob stayed in Haran and worked for his mother's brother, Laban. One day he told Laban that he loved Rachel, his daughter, and offered to work for seven years to earn her hand in marriage. Laban agreed to this.

It was the custom, however, for the older daughter to marry before the younger. So when the wedding night arrived and Jacob was to go to Rachel in the dark, Laban swapped Rachel for Leah, his oldest daughter.

When Jacob discovered what had happened he was furious—so Laban suggested that Jacob should finish the wedding week with Leah and then he could marry Rachel too. Although this would be in return for another seven years' work, Jacob was happy to agree.

People usually sat around a low table on cushions, mats or stools to eat a wedding feast. Fruits such as melons, figs, grapes, pomegranates and olives were eaten, as were fish, meat and bread. Figs were made into cakes. Wine was served in jars.

A WEDDING FEAST
A bride in later times would wear a headband of coins at her wedding.

The groom went with his friends to collect the bride from her house.

Bride's house

INSTRUMENTS PLAYED AT A WEDDING FEAST

A drum

A flute

This chart is a family tree. It shows the most important descendants (children, grandchildren, great grandchildren and so on) of Terah who was descended from Noah. The family tree helps show at a glance, for example, the names of Jacob's twelve sons—from whom the twelve tribes of Israel descended. Jacob's name was changed to Israel by God and his people became known as Israelites.

Terah

Nahor — married Hagar (handmaiden) ══ Abraham ══ married Sarah — Haran

Bethuel — Ishmael — married Rebekah ══ Isaac — Iscah — Milcah — Lot

Laban — Rebekah — Esau — Ammon — Moab

Leah — Rachel — married Zilpah (handmaiden) ══ married Leah ══ Jacob (Israel) ══ married Rachel ══ married Bilhah (handmaiden)

Gad, Asher — Reuben, Simeon, Levi, Judah, Issachar, Zebulun — Joseph — Benjamin — Dan, Naphtali

Ephraim, Manasseh

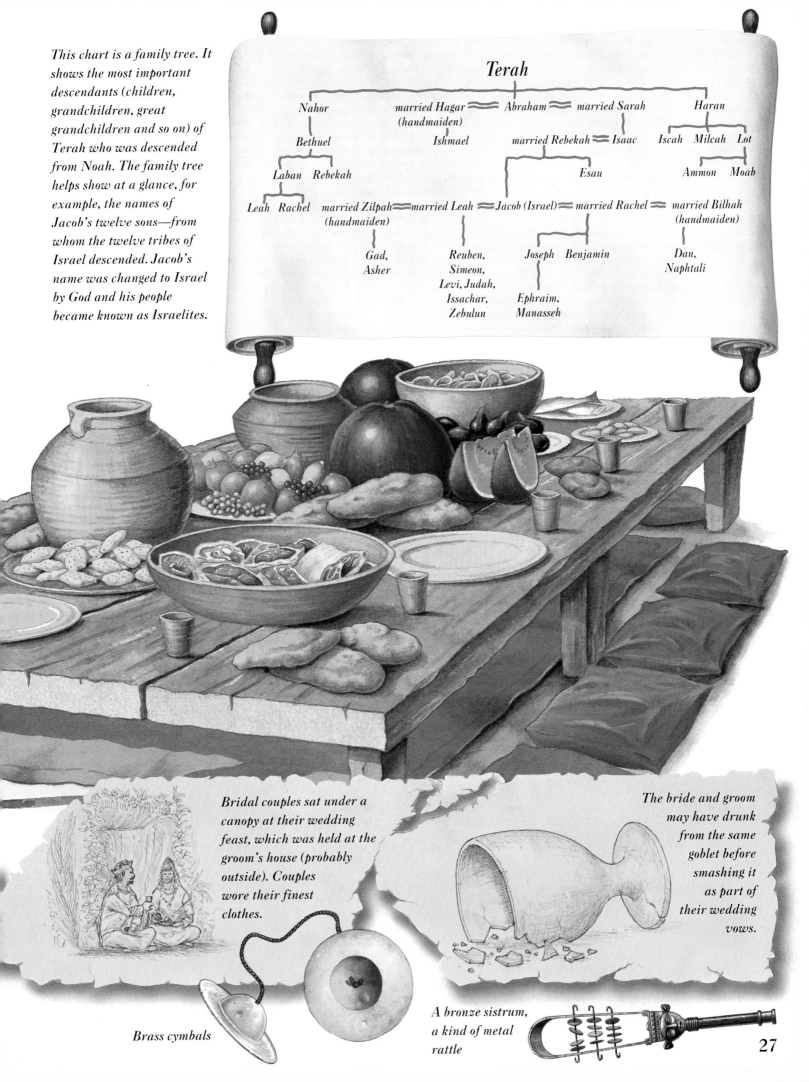

Bridal couples sat under a canopy at their wedding feast, which was held at the groom's house (probably outside). Couples wore their finest clothes.

Brass cymbals

The bride and groom may have drunk from the same goblet before smashing it as part of their wedding vows.

A bronze sistrum, a kind of metal rattle

27

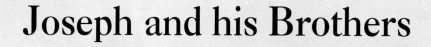

THE ISRAELITES IN EGYPT

Cumin

Flax

Stories of a nation without a country

Joseph and his Brothers

Jacob's wives bore him many sons, but one of them, named Joseph, was his favourite child because he was born to Rachel and Jacob in their old age. Jacob decided to weave Joseph a beautiful coat.

One night Joseph dreamed that the sun, moon and eleven stars bowed down to him. When he told his family about the dream they were furious.

They thought the dream was meant to tell the future: the sun and the moon were Joseph's father and mother and the stars were his eleven brothers. Jacob said to him sternly, 'Do you think we are all going to bow down to you?' Joseph's brothers were already jealous. Now they were so angry they began to plot against him.

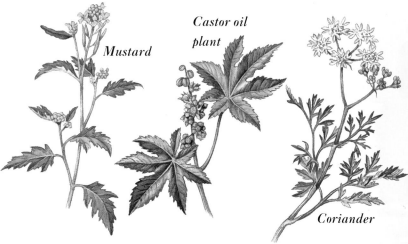

Mustard

Castor oil plant

Coriander

Cumin, coriander and mustard are some of the kinds of spices carried by traders in biblical times. They also traded oils, such as castor oil, and linen—a type of cloth made of fibres taken from the flax plant.

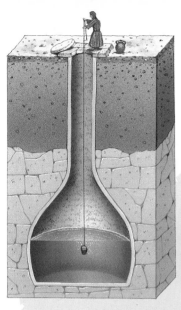

A cistern was a small reservoir for storing rainwater. It was dug deep in the ground to stop the water from evaporating in the sun.

One day Jacob sent Joseph to the fields where his brothers were grazing sheep. When they saw him alone without his father to protect him, they decided that this was their chance for revenge. 'Let's kill him and throw him into this dry cistern. We can say that a wild animal got him.'

When Joseph arrived they took off his special coat and threw him into the cistern. Laughing, they sat down to eat.

Then the brothers saw a camel caravan of Ishmaelites coming toward them. One brother suggested selling Joseph as a slave to the traders, who were taking spices to Egypt. They pulled Joseph out of the cistern and gave him to the Ishmaelites for twenty shekels. The average price for a slave was thirty shekels so Joseph was a bargain. Then they stained his coat with the blood of a dead goat to make it look as though he had been attacked by a wild animal.

They took the coat back to their father. Jacob recognized it immediately and threw up his hands in horror. 'My son's coat—he has been eaten by an animal!' Jacob mourned Joseph for a long time and refused to be comforted by his other children.

Shekels were stone weights.

Camel caravans travelled along trade routes between the north and Egypt. They carried important spices used in cooking food and making perfume. There were many traders in this area buying and selling silver, iron, slaves, tin, lead, bronze, ivory and horses.

Joseph and the Great Famine

When the Ishmaelites arrived in Egypt, they sold Joseph to Potiphar, the captain of Pharaoh's army. Potiphar liked Joseph and appointed him to look after his house. But Potiphar's wife told her husband that Joseph had tried to attack her. Potiphar was furious and threw Joseph into Pharaoh's prison.

Once again Joseph was a prisoner. But he could still tell the future by interpreting dreams. He correctly predicted that one of the prisoners would be restored to his place as Pharaoh's servant. Some time later, when Pharaoh was trying to find out the meaning of a dream, the servant remembered Joseph and told Pharaoh. Pharaoh called him out of prison. 'In my dream,' said Pharaoh, 'I was standing on the bank of the River Nile and seven fat cows came out of the river. They

were followed by seven thin cows who ate the fat ones, and yet looked no fatter.'

Joseph explained that the seven fat cows were seven years of good harvest when the Egyptians would have lots of food. But then seven years of famine would follow. Joseph said this was God's way of warning Pharaoh of the coming disaster and he advised Pharaoh to start storing grain for the bad years.

Pharaoh accepted Joseph's wise words and made him governor (vizier) of all Egypt. Joseph was given gold rings, necklaces and fine robes. He married the daughter of the Egyptian priest of Heliopolis. He also began overseeing the collection and storage of grain from the fields by the River Nile for the years of famine to come.

An Egyptian vizier was one of the highest officials in the land. He would have worn expensive clothes and jewels to show his status. Wigs made of human hair were worn by rich Egyptians. The wigs were stuck on with beeswax.

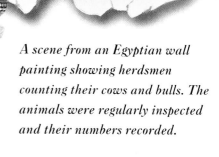

A scene from an Egyptian wall painting showing herdsmen counting their cows and bulls. The animals were regularly inspected and their numbers recorded.

A model wooden granary that was found inside an Egyptian tomb. It shows a scribe recording the amount of grain before it is stored in three large bins. In the foreground a woman is grinding barley on a stone.

After seven years the harvests started to fail and people from every part of Egypt began coming to Joseph for the grain he had saved. But as each year passed the famine grew worse, and people flooded into Egypt from all the surrounding countries.

One day, as Joseph was giving out grain, he recognized his brothers in the crowd. Jacob must have sent them to Egypt because of the famine at home. They did not recognize Joseph, so he pretended not to know them. Joseph spoke sternly to them and accused them of spying. In fear they said they weren't spies, just twelve brothers; one had died, and the youngest stayed behind in Canaan. Joseph ordered them to fetch this brother, as only then would he believe them. They returned with their youngest brother, Benjamin, who was the only other child of Joseph's mother. They gave Joseph gifts and bowed down before him.

Joseph could not keep his secret any longer. He ordered all the Egyptian officials out of the room and said to his brothers, 'I am your brother Joseph whom you sold into slavery.' They were terrified of what he would do, but Joseph still loved his brothers and forgave them. He told them to go back to Canaan and bring their father Jacob and their families back to Egypt to live with him.

Joseph went out in a fast chariot to meet them when they returned. The moment Jacob saw his long-lost son he wept with joy.

Barley and wheat were grown in ancient Egypt.

Wheat

Barley

Pharaoh's Slaves

Three hundred years after the death of Joseph, the Israelites still lived in Egypt. But times had changed, and a new dynasty of pharaohs had forgotten the days when Joseph saved the country from starvation.

The new Pharaoh planned to construct many new buildings. He wanted to build a grand palace for himself and huge grain stores in case of another famine. He also wanted to control the growing number of Israelites, so he made them his slaves.

Pharaoh's slave masters treated the Israelites very harshly. Many of them had to work in the fields during the hottest part of the day or make and haul bricks to build Pharaoh's city.

Still Pharaoh feared that the Israelites might gain power. So he said to the Israelite midwives, 'When you help an Israelite woman to have a baby, take note whether it is a boy or a girl: if it is a boy, kill him, if it is a girl,

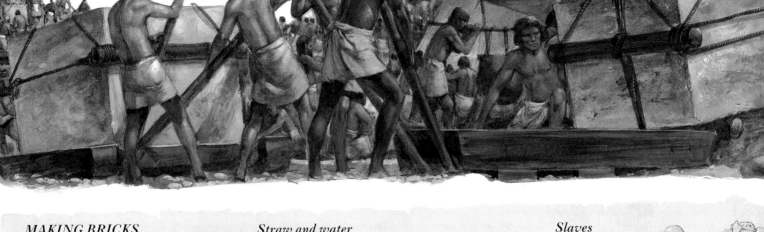

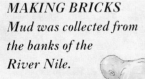

MAKING BRICKS
Mud was collected from the banks of the River Nile.

Straw and water were added to the mud. The straw made the mixture stronger.

Slaves transported the mixture to the moulding and drying area.

An inkwell and reed pens

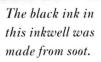

The black ink in this inkwell was made from soot.

let her live.' The midwives were afraid of Pharaoh, but they feared God more. So they disobeyed Pharaoh and pretended that all the Israelites' children were born before they could get there.

When Pharaoh realized what was happening he ordered all his people to throw every new-born Israelite boy into the river.

The tombs and palaces of the pharaohs often had walls decorated with stories told in Egyptian writing. The writing above tells the story of a hunt. Writing was invented in Babylonia, near where Abraham was born, but long before his time. The idea of writing then came to Egypt. The Egyptians made up their own language of picture signs known as hieroglyphics. People wrote on tablets of clay or with a reed pen on papyrus paper.

A reed pen

Nearly everybody in Egypt worked for Pharaoh. These slaves are building part of a temple complex. Some people worked as builders, others as miners or stone quarriers. Yet others repaired the canals and fences that were damaged when the River Nile burst its banks each year.

Papyrus reeds

The bricks were left out in the sun to dry.

A slave carried the dried bricks to the building site using a sling attached to a yoke.

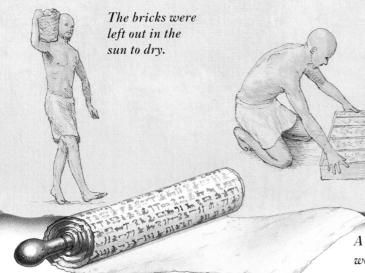

A papyrus scroll rolled around wood. 'Paper' was made from papyrus reeds.

Moses and the Burning Bush

An ancient Egyptian board game known as senet. It is made of ivory and ebony (a type of wood) and belonged to a pharaoh.

During the time of Pharaoh's order that all male Israelite children should be thrown into the river, a husband and wife from the family of Levi hid their baby boy for three months. The time came when they could not hide him any longer, so they put him in a waterproof basket and placed it in the reeds of the River Nile.

The baby's sister hid there to see what would happen. Pharaoh's daughter spotted the child and felt sorry for him. His sister came out of hiding and offered to find an Israelite woman to nurse him. Pharaoh's daughter agreed, and the girl

returned with the child's mother. Pharaoh's daughter told her to nurse the baby, without realizing that she was his real mother. When the child was older he was taken to Pharaoh's daughter, who named him Moses, which means 'drawn out of the water'. Moses was brought up in the Egyptian palace.

When Moses was a grown man he saw the suffering of the Israelites, his own people, as they worked for Pharaoh. One day Moses saw an Egyptian beating an Israelite, and in his rage he killed the Egyptian and hid his body in the sand. Then he fled to the land of Midian.

As he sat down by a well after his journey, seven daughters of a Midianite priest came along to give

Papyrus reeds were used to make many things, including baskets and mats. The basket that Moses was found in would probably have been shaped like a boat.

34

It was common for foreign children to be taken into the Egyptian royal household and educated, taught sports and board games. Children played with wooden toys like these.

A spinning top made of quartz

A toy cat or lion

A wooden toy horse

A doll with wool for hair

that although the bush was on fire, it was not destroyed. 'Moses, Moses,' cried out a voice. 'Do not come any closer, but take off your sandals for this is holy ground.' Moses quickly took them off and hid his face in fear.

God spoke from the bush, 'I have seen the misery of my people in Egypt who are slaves of Pharaoh. I will take them to a land flowing with milk and honey. I am sending you to save my people, the Israelites.'

Terrified, Moses said that he was not strong enough to fight Pharaoh. 'Please send someone else,' he begged. God said he would enable Moses to perform miracles with his staff and would send his brother Aaron to help him. God told Moses he must travel to Egypt and force Pharaoh to 'let my people go'.

water to their sheep. Some local shepherds started bothering the girls and tried to drive their sheep away. Moses came to their rescue and the shepherds left. The girls were so grateful they took Moses back to meet their father, Jethro. Moses stayed for forty years, married one of the priest's daughters, Zipporah, and had two sons.

One day while Moses was out looking after Jethro's flock, he came to Mount Horeb, the holy mountain. A bush on the far side of the desert caught his attention and started to burn. Moses saw

This Egyptian wand may be similar to the staff God gave Moses. It is made of ivory and is decorated with pictures of animals and Egyptian goddesses. These wands were used by the Egyptians to draw a circle around their beds at night. It was thought that this would protect the sleeper from snakes and scorpions.

The Plagues

Moses and Aaron travelled to Egypt. At their meeting with Pharaoh, Aaron's miracle staff turned into a snake as a sign of God's power. But Pharaoh's magicians did the same trick.

When Moses and Aaron next went to see Pharaoh, Aaron touched the Nile with his staff. Immediately the river turned to blood. All the fish died, and the water smelled so bad that the Egyptians could not drink it. But this plague did not work because the Pharaoh did not care that his people had no water to drink.

Seven days later, Aaron stretched his staff over Egypt's canals and ponds. Masses of frogs started to leap on to the land. They jumped into people's homes and into Pharaoh's palace. Frogs were everywhere, even in the bedroom of Pharaoh's daughter. Pharaoh begged Moses to take them away, but when God killed the frogs, Pharaoh went back on his promise to let the Israelites leave.

God brought more plagues on the Egyptians. He turned the soil into gnats which attacked people and animals. Swarms of flies then flew into Pharaoh's palace. God diseased all the cattle, and then sent a plague of boils to cover the skin of the Egyptians and their animals. Pharaoh was still stubborn, and so God sent three more plagues on him.

A terrible hailstorm destroyed the animals and the crops in the fields. Then swarms of locusts covered the land and ate what little was left after the hail. Finally, the whole land became completely dark for three days. But God left light where the Israelites lived so that Pharaoh could see that God had chosen them as his people.

Pharaoh begged Moses to tell God to end each new plague. Each time Pharaoh promised that he would let the Israelites go once the plague had ended. But Pharaoh always forgot his promise.

God decided to

A small stela, or gravestone, showing the figure of the Egyptian god Horus, standing on crocodiles. He is holding snakes, scorpions and gazelles in his hands. The stela was thought to have magical powers to protect people against these 'evil' creatures. The Egyptians believed in magic, and there are many tales of famous Egyptian magicians, such as Pharaoh's magicians in this story.

send one last plague to Egypt. Moses told the Israelites how to prepare, in order to avoid the final plague. On the evening before the last plague, every Israelite family killed a young lamb and roasted it over the fire. Using bunches of hyssop they painted lambs' blood on the doors of their houses to show that they were Israelites and not Egyptians. They then ate their meal of lamb and flat, unleavened bread and waited inside until morning.

At midnight, an angel sent by God went through the land killing all the eldest children of Egypt, including Pharaoh's own son. The angel avoided the doors of houses marked with blood. He knew they were the houses of the Israelites and passed over them. The loud crying and screaming of the Egyptians filled the night air.

Pharaoh called Moses and said, 'Enough! Go from this land of Egypt.' So the Israelites left the land where they had been slaves for so long.

The meal that the Israelites ate on their last night in Egypt is known as the Passover because God passed over their houses and saved the Israelite children from death.

The plant hyssop was a type of herb that grew in the region. The Israelites used bunches of hyssop to brush their doors with lambs' blood as a sign to the angel.

The Israelites lived separately from the Egyptians in cramped, single-storey houses. The houses were built of bricks made from mud (see pages 32–33), collected by the Israelites from the Nile delta—the triangular area of land formed by mud where the River Nile reaches the sea. Their homes were situated in Goshen, not far from the Nile delta.

The Exodus

On the night of the Passover, the Israelites were driven out of Egypt by the angry Pharaoh. Their leaving of Egypt came to be known as the Exodus. About half a million families left Egypt with their cattle, sheep and goats. They travelled from Rameses to Succoth without stopping. By day God led them with a pillar of cloud, by night with a pillar of fire.

Eventually they came to the sea and camped because they thought that they were safe from Pharaoh. But when Pharaoh heard that the Israelites had fled, he changed his mind. 'After them, you fools!' he barked out at his officers. 'Do not let the Israelites get away.'

Pharaoh's cavalry rushed off in pursuit of the Israelites and quickly caught up. In terror, the Israelites saw the Egyptians on the horizon. They cried out to Moses, 'Have you brought us into the desert to die?

Better to be a slave in Egypt than dead in the desert!' 'Don't be afraid,' Moses replied, confident that God would save them.

Moses stretched his staff out across the sea in front of him and God held back the water, allowing the Israelites to cross. But when Pharaoh's army tried to cross, their chariots swerved on the mud. Moses stretched

FOOD IN THE DESERT
God provided the Israelites with manna, which may have been the sweet drops of fluid secreted by insects living on tamarisk trees. The drops fell to the ground and were then collected.

Quails were eaten when they fell from the sky exhausted by the heat.

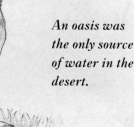

An oasis was the only source of water in the desert.

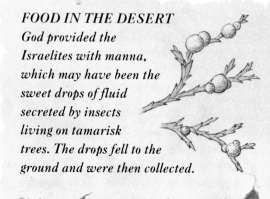

HUNTING WEAPONS

A spear

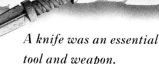

A knife was an essential tool and weapon.

out his staff over the sea again, and the water rolled back like a huge tidal wave. All of the Egyptians were drowned. The Israelites, safe on the other side of the sea, looked back in amazement at their escape.

After they had fled from Egypt, the Israelites wandered in the deserts of Sinai for forty years.

MEDITERRANEAN SEA

CANAAN

Mount Nebo

DEAD SEA

Rameses

EGYPT

Succoth

A trader on a camel

Israelites fought the Canaanites

An Egyptian chariot

SINAI

Israelites

The Israelites camped in the desert

MIDIAN

GULF OF SUEZ

GULF OF AQABA

Mount Sinai

RED SEA

A map showing the probable route of the Exodus. It is thought that the sea the Israelites crossed may have been an area of marshy land, called the 'Reed Sea', between the Gulf of Suez and the Mediterranean Sea. The Israelites then camped in the desert for forty years before invading Canaan, the Promised Land, from the east. Earlier, some Israelites had disobeyed Moses and attempted to invade Canaan from the south. They were defeated and sadly returned to the desert.

The chariot was the most important part of the Egyptian army. Chariots were perfect for chasing the enemies of Pharaoh and also for long-distance marches and wars.

Dates and figs were eaten.

Gazelles were hunted with a bow and arrow.

A fig

Dates

A bow and arrows

A sling

39

The Promised Land

Stories of how a people found their homeland

Moses and the Ten Commandments

Three months after their escape from Egypt, the Israelites came to the Sinai desert and camped at the foot of Mount Sinai. They had no food so God gave them manna to eat.

God called from the mountain, commanding Moses to speak to him. He told Moses that he would appear in three days' time and that the Israelites should pray, wash their clothes and on no account set foot on the mountain. On the third day thunder roared and everyone in the camp rushed to Mount Sinai to receive God's law.

Moses climbed up the mountain. The Israelites waited for six days and then God spoke his commandments:

'I am the Lord your God, who brought you out of Egypt.

'You shall have no other gods but me.

'You shall not make a false god out of anything on the earth or in the sea. I am a jealous God and will punish those who hate me.

'Do not use my name in vain.

'Remember the Sabbath day and keep it holy. Work for six days, but not on the seventh because God made Heaven and Earth in six days

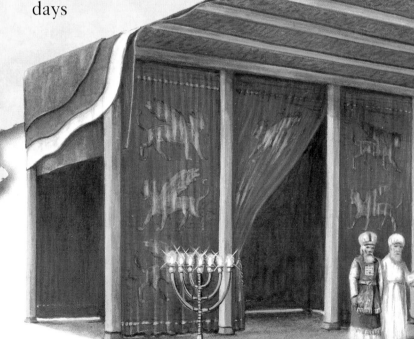

The Israelites spoke Hebrew. This is a fragment of Phoenician script which was very like the Hebrew script. The writing on the stone tablets given to Moses may have looked something like this.

and rested on the seventh day.

'Do as your father and mother tell you.

'You shall not kill anyone.

'You shall not take another man's wife, or another woman's husband.

'You shall not steal.

'You shall not lie about your neighbour.

'You shall not want anything that is your neighbour's.'

Moses stayed on the mountain for forty days. While he was there, the Israelites asked Moses' brother Aaron, the high priest, to make them a new god. They gave Aaron their gold Egyptian earrings which he melted in a fire to form a single block in the shape of a calf. The Israelites worshipped the calf.

Moses returned from Mount Sinai with the commandments written on two stone tablets. When he saw the Israelites praising the calf he smashed the tablets. The next day Moses climbed the mountain to ask forgiveness for the Israelites. He returned with new stone tablets as a record of God's laws.

Aramaic and Hebrew were alphabets written by the people of the ancient Near East. In this table the letters of the two alphabets are compared to the modern Roman alphabet we use.

ARAMAIC (ELEPHANTINE)	HEBREW CURSIVE	MODERN ROMAN
		A
		B
		C
		D
		E
		F
		Z
		H
		I
		K
		L
		M
		N
		O
		P
		Q
		R
		S
		T

Along with the ten commandments, God gave the Israelites instructions on how to worship. They had to construct a tent, called a tabernacle, as a meeting place. The tent was made of layers of animal skins covering a wooden frame. It was hung with curtains of finely woven linen. The holy stone tablets were kept in a wooden chest covered with gold called the ark.

The Fall of Jericho

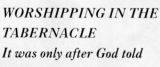

A ram's horn

The Israelites wandered in the desert for forty years before they finally reached Canaan, the Promised Land. Moses climbed up a high mountain, called Mount Nebo, and looked over the whole country. Then, at the age of one hundred and twenty, he died and was buried on the mountain.

A man named Joshua became the leader of the Israelites. He was determined to take the land of Canaan which God meant for the Israelites. So he sent two men to Canaan as spies. They stayed in the house of a woman named Rahab in the city of Jericho. When Jericho's king found out about the spies he sent soldiers after them. But Rahab hid the spies and told the soldiers that the men had left. They then escaped over the city wall.

Joshua then led his soldiers against Jericho. They were followed by seven priests carrying the ark, the wooden chest that held the commandments.

Soldiers from the twelve tribes of Israel marched around Jericho for seven days. On the seventh day the priests blasted on their horns, the Israelites began to shout and the walls of Jericho crumbled.

WORSHIPPING IN THE TABERNACLE
It was only after God told Moses how his people were to praise him that the Israelites had a formal system of worship.

The priests would sacrifice an animal, sprinkle its blood on the altar and wash it in the basin. It was then burned.

The altar used to burn offerings.

Washing basin or laver

Altar for burning incense

The Israelites rushed in through the gaps in the walls, set all the houses on fire and killed everyone in the city. Only Rahab and her family were spared. The ark was then carried into the city as the Israelites celebrated their first victory over the people of Canaan.

Before they conquered Jericho, the Israelites fought battles with the peoples who lived east of the River Jordan. Some of their land was captured by the Israelites and became part of the territory divided up among the twelve tribes of Israel.

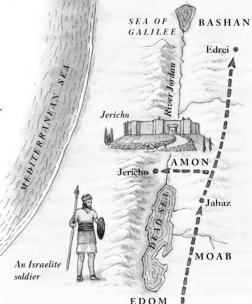

An Israelite soldier

The Israelites invaded Canaan from the east. After crossing the River Jordan they came to Jericho (left). Jericho is perhaps the oldest city in the world, in existence since before 6000 B.C.

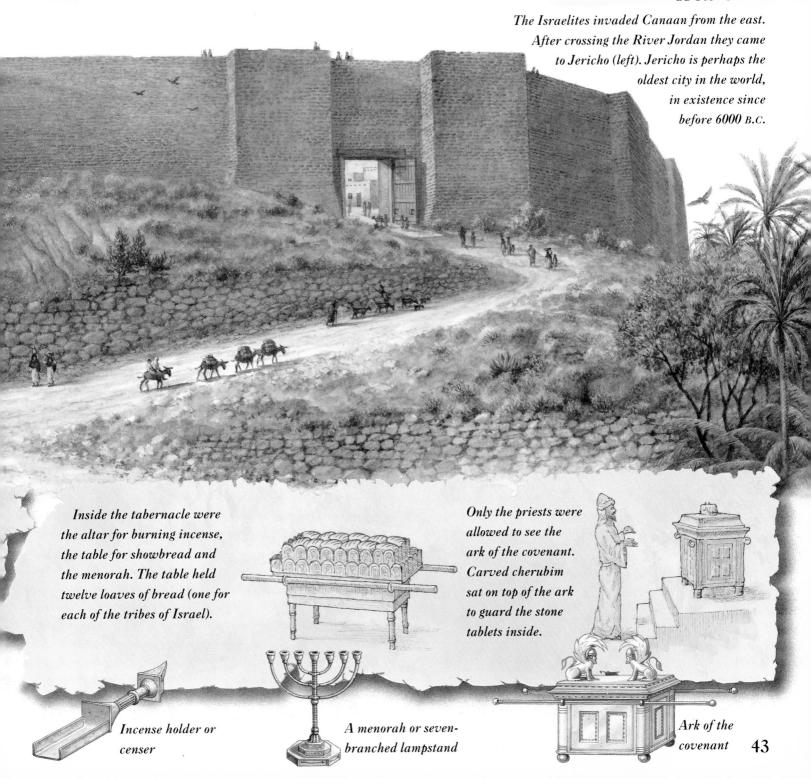

Inside the tabernacle were the altar for burning incense, the table for showbread and the menorah. The table held twelve loaves of bread (one for each of the tribes of Israel).

Only the priests were allowed to see the ark of the covenant. Carved cherubim sat on top of the ark to guard the stone tablets inside.

Incense holder or censer

A menorah or seven-branched lampstand

Ark of the covenant

43

Deborah the Prophetess

After the fall of Jericho, one city after another in Canaan was captured by the Israelites. They divided their army into groups that went to conquer cities in the south and north. The Canaanites were afraid of these people of God—how could they be defeated when they were helped by God himself?

It was not long before the Israelites had conquered nearly all of Canaan. They divided the land among themselves so that each tribe had its own territory, except the Levites whom God had made a tribe of priests. It was their job to take care of Israel's religious life. Israel would only continue to

The Levite priests wore white robes with a sash tied at the waist. They performed the religious duties at the tabernacle. The priests were also teachers and acted as judges.

receive God's blessing if the Israelites obeyed the ten commandments.

But the Israelites did not always keep God's laws. They disobeyed God and had to ask him for forgiveness.

One cruel Canaanite king, named Jabin, ruled the Israelites for twenty years. Israel did not have its own king, but was ruled by a warrior, who led them into battle and also acted as a judge whenever there were arguments between people or tribes.

One of the judges was named Deborah. The Israelites came to the place where she sat,

On a Canaanite chariot one man held the reins of the horses while the other shot arrows at the enemy. A quiver for the arrows was fitted to the side of the chariot. Infantrymen followed on foot carrying shields and sickle-shaped swords.

The Israelites were no longer wandering nomads. They gave up their tents and built their own homes. They became a nation of farmers, growing fruit and vegetables. Most Israelites had to settle in the mountains because they could not drive out the Canaanites who lived in the valleys.

called Deborah's palm, and asked her what they should do because King Jabin had taken control of all their trade routes and was threatening to massacre the northern tribes of Israel. Deborah sent for her commander, Barak, and told him of a vision she had received from God: Barak would defeat Jabin's great army of thousands of soldiers and nine hundred iron chariots with just ten thousand men. Barak was nervous, but he agreed to follow Deborah's advice.

Barak and Deborah went to the top of Mount Tabor with their army of ten thousand foot soldiers and camped. On high ground they were safer from attack. When the time was right, Deborah gave the signal, and Barak and his men charged down the hillside. It suddenly started to pour with rain, and the river at the bottom of the mountain began to flood. Its banks overflowed and turned the battlefield to mud. The wheels of King Jabin's chariots stuck in the mud, making the charioteers sitting targets. The Israelites charged and Jabin's army was slaughtered.

But Jabin's commander, Sisera, escaped. He took shelter in a house in a nearby village. The people of the house said they would keep watch for him. But when he was asleep, the woman of the house took a tent peg and hammered it through his head into the ground.

Deborah's palm would have been a date palm, a tall tree with leaves two metres long.

45

Samson in the Temple

About fifty years after the death of Deborah, a new enemy, the Philistines, arose against the Israelites. They were also known as the 'sea peoples' because they lived by the Mediterranean Sea. They were a powerful nation, with weapons made of iron, and they defeated the Israelites in battle for many years.

One day a woman from the tribe of Dan gave birth to a special boy. An angel had appeared to the woman saying that her son would grow up to lead the Israelites to victory against the Philistines. But this was on one condition: that he never cut his hair.

The boy was called Samson, and he grew up to be very strong. He could beat the Philistines single-handed. Once

A Philistine warrior

An Israelite warrior

Both the Israelite and Philistine warriors wore simple garments of shirts and kilts.

he killed a thousand Philistines using only the jawbone of a donkey.

Samson spent a lot of time in Philistine country. There he met and fell in love with a woman called Delilah. The Philistines promised to pay Delilah eleven hundred pieces of

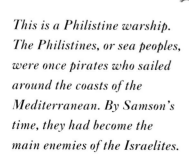

This is a Philistine warship. The Philistines, or sea peoples, were once pirates who sailed around the coasts of the Mediterranean. By Samson's time, they had become the main enemies of the Israelites.

This is a Philistine temple from Tell Qasile in northern Philistia (an area by the Mediterranean Sea). The temple is smaller than the one Samson destroyed. The main hall had pillars of cedarwood and seats around the walls. A statue of the Philistine god would have stood on the raised platform in the corner. The roof was supported by wooden beams.

silver to discover the secret of Samson's strength. At first Samson refused to reveal his secret, then he finally gave in and told Delilah, 'If my head were shaved, my strength would leave me.'

Delilah whispered to one of the house guards to cut off Samson's hair while he slept. When his head was completely shaved, she shouted 'Samson, the Philistines are attacking!' He

The Philistines are thought to have come originally from the Mycenaean culture of south and central Greece. This is a Mycenaean jug, an amphora, from about 1400 B.C., decorated with a drawing of an octopus.

jumped up and ran out to fight, but his strength had gone. The Philistines grabbed him, gouged out his eyes, and took him to prison.

Some time later, the Philistines were in the temple of Dagon worshipping their god when they asked for Samson to be brought in for their amusement.

By this time, Samson's hair had grown back, and he prayed that his strength would also be restored. When the Philistines brought him out, he stood between two pillars of the temple and pushed with all his might. The pillars gave way and the roof came crashing down, burying all the Philistines alive—and Samson too.

The Story of Ruth

At the time when famine spread across Judah in southern Israel, a man called Elimelech, his wife Naomi and their two sons moved from their home of Bethlehem to Moab, east of the Dead Sea.

Not long after arriving, Elimelech died. In time, his sons married Orpah and Ruth, two women from Moab. After ten years another tragedy struck—Naomi's two sons died. Since Naomi had lost both her husband and sons, she decided to return to her relatives in Bethlehem. She told Orpah and Ruth to stay in Moab and go back to their mothers' houses. Orpah agreed but Ruth said she would go with Naomi to Bethlehem and accept the will of God.

Naomi and Ruth returned to Bethlehem during the barley harvest. Ruth went out into the fields and joined the women gathering the barley. The fields were owned by Boaz, a wealthy relative of Naomi and Elimelech, and he was kind to Ruth.

Naomi told Ruth to make herself look beautiful and go to where Boaz was working. 'Don't let him

HARVESTING
Reapers in the fields cut off the tops of the barley with sickles. Women picked up the barley left by the cutters. This was known as 'gleaning'.

The sheaves of barley were heaped into a basket and pressed down by two men with a long rod.

TOOLS FOR FARMING

An Egyptian sickle with flint cutting edge

A mattock, a type of hoe

An iron-bladed sickle from 1000 B.C.

48

A diagram of the Israelites' farming year. It shows at what time of year different agricultural activities took place. We can see: ploughing the land (1), sowing the seed (2), growing the crops (3), harvesting: citrus fruits (4), flax (5), barley (6), wheat (7), grapes (8), olives (9), dates (10), and storing the produce (11).

recognize you while he is eating and drinking. But when he lies down, go and turn back the covering at his feet and lie down.'

Ruth followed Naomi's advice and, during the night, Boaz woke up to discover that there was a woman lying at his feet. Ruth told Boaz who she was and asked him to spread his cloak over her as a sign that he would marry her. But Boaz said there was another man who, as a closer relative, had first choice of her. When a woman's husband died, it was the custom for the husband's brother or nearest relative to marry the widow.

The next morning Boaz offered Ruth to the closer relative. To show that he was not interested, the man offered Boaz his sandal, a sign that he was passing the opportunity to Boaz. Boaz received Ruth with open arms. In time, Ruth gave birth to a boy called Obed who grew up to be the father of Jesse and the grandfather of David, Israel's greatest king.

Oxen dragged a threshing sledge. It had flints fixed along its underside to cut up the straw and separate it from the grain.

The farmer used a large wooden fork called a winnowing fan to throw the separated grain and straw into the air. The straw was blown away by the wind and the grain collected with a shovel.

A wooden shovel

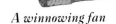

A winnowing fan

49

David's Kingdom

Slingstones

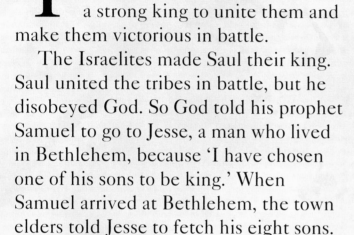
David's sling

David and Goliath

The time of the judges' rule was over. Now the Israelites needed a strong king to unite them and make them victorious in battle.

The Israelites made Saul their king. Saul united the tribes in battle, but he disobeyed God. So God told his prophet Samuel to go to Jesse, a man who lived in Bethlehem, because 'I have chosen one of his sons to be king.' When Samuel arrived at Bethlehem, the town elders told Jesse to fetch his eight sons.

It was the youngest son, the shepherd boy David, whom God told Samuel he had chosen. David became a musician and page in Saul's court.

The Israelites and the Philistines were fighting at this time. At one battle the Philistines and Israelites lined up on the opposite sides of a valley. The Philistines' greatest warrior, Goliath, shouted to the Israelites to pick one man to fight him. Whoever won

the fight would win the battle for his people. The Israelites were terrified of Goliath who was three metres tall. Only David came forward.

Saul, who did not know that David was chosen as his successor, said, 'You are just a shepherd. You won't stand a chance!' But David replied, 'When a bear attacks my sheep, I rescue the sheep from its mouth, and kill the bear. This Philistine will be like the bear who has come to attack my people.' Saul thought and then said, 'Go and fight Goliath, and God be with you.' David took five smooth stones and a sling.

When Goliath saw this boy he thought the Israelites had gone mad. As David moved closer to Goliath, he slung a stone and hit him in the forehead, knocking him dead. David ran up to Goliath, took his sword, and cut off his head.

The higher-ranking Philistine soldiers wore protective coats of mail. Mail is made of small plates of bronze hung on woollen mesh, like the tiles on the roof of a house.

The Israelites (below) would have been armed for battle with slings and slingstones, axes, bows and arrows, swords and spears. The Philistines (left) had chariots and horses, whereas the Israelites only had foot soldiers. Although the Philistines usually beat the Israelites in battle, the Israelites won some important fights by using clever tactics.

The Capture of Jerusalem

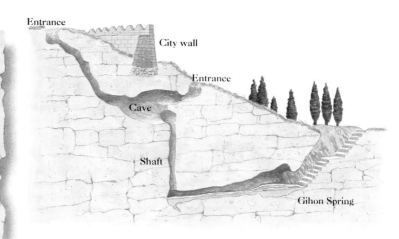

David became a clever soldier. He pretended to be a friend of the Philistines so they would send him out to fight their enemies and bring them back what he had captured. He usually defeated these enemies, but he only handed over enough of the booty to keep the Philistines satisfied. David kept the rest and gave it to his own soldiers.

In time, David built up a large army of his own. He moved his headquarters away from the Philistines to the town of Hebron, high in the hills of Judah. David became very popular with the people of Judah, who remembered how he had killed the giant Goliath and could see that he still protected them from their enemies. When Saul died in a battle, the people of Judah made David their king.

This diagram shows how David captured the city of Jerusalem. It is most likely that David's men discovered a tunnel going into the side of the hill below the city wall which joined another tunnel running from an underground pool.

David was thirty years old when he became king, and he ruled Judah for seven and a half years. He was very successful and won nearly every battle he fought. The elders of Israel came to Hebron to meet him and crown him king of all Israel.

When the Philistines heard this news, and realized that David had betrayed them, they marched against him. David sent out scouts who saw the Philistines coming. So he commanded his troops to make a

Before David conquered Jerusalem the city was called Jebus. The inhabitants were the only Canaanites whom the Israelites had not conquered. The city was difficult to attack because it was built on top of a hill.

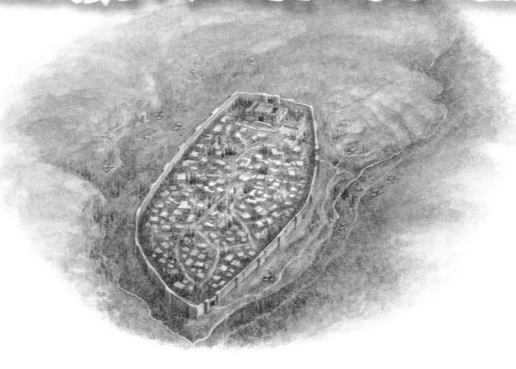

surprise attack. The Israelites hid in the woods and waited. When the Philistine army passed by, the Israelites ambushed them and slaughtered them all.

Now that David was king of all Israel he needed a suitable capital. There was one city, set on seven hills and held by the Jebusites, which the Israelites had never been able to capture because of its strong defensive position. It was the city of Jerusalem and would be a perfect capital for Israel.

Jerusalem was thought to be impossible to conquer because of its high stone walls. But David discovered a tunnel which led from a water pool outside the city under the city wall. The Jebusites used this tunnel to fetch their water. David's men scrambled along the tunnel and climbed up into the city and captured it. They let the Jebusites live because they had surrendered.

When David's friend, the king of Tyre (a port on the Mediterranean coast north of Israel),

The stonemasons from Tyre cut out large rectangular blocks of limestone to build King David's new palace. The limestone was cut in the quarry while it was still soft because it hardens when exposed to hot, dry air.

The kind of harp played in Israel was small enough to carry. The harpist often played and walked at the same time. This harp is called a kinnor. David would have played one like this when he was a boy tending his father's sheep on the hills.

heard that David had taken Jerusalem, he sent his best carpenters and stonemasons to build David a royal palace. Everyone was excited and sang and danced through the streets. All the elders of Israel assembled to celebrate. Then they held a ceremony in which the holy ark was carried up to the city. David proudly led the procession, dancing in front of the ark all the way up the hill and through the city gates. By bringing the ark to Jerusalem, the Israelites believed that they were bringing God into their city.

53

Solomon's Temple

When King David died, his son Solomon became the new king of the Israelites. Solomon had a peaceful reign because David had defeated all of Israel's many enemies.

Solomon spent his time building palaces, a fleet of ships and even a whole city. But the most precious place of all was the one God commanded Solomon to build. It was a temple for the people of Israel to worship in.

Solomon used the finest materials to build his temple. Wood from the cedar and cypress trees of Phoenicia was transported over 160 kilometres to Jerusalem to make the roof and line the temple walls. Craftsmen laid gold in the doors and made columns of bronze. The walls of the temple were made of blocks of stone.

After seven years of building, everything was finished. People came from all over the country to see the new temple and to give thanks to God.

The bronze sea

The altar

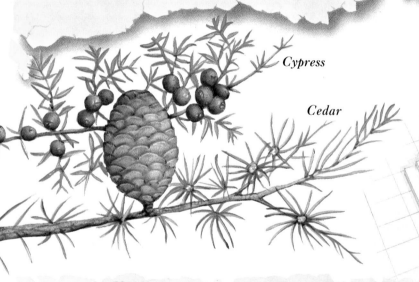

Cypress

Cedar

BUILDING THE TEMPLE
Logs were loaded on to Solomon's ships.

TOOLS FOR BUILDING

54

A tool for shaving wood

Nails

An adze

A ram carved in gold. The Israelites used to offer rams to thank God for helping them. The Israelites believed that the sweet smell of roast lamb rising to heaven made God happy.

Solomon's high priest wore fine colourful robes. On his chest he wore a linen breastplate with twelve precious stones set into it. Each stone represented one of the twelve tribes of Israel which had settled in Canaan.

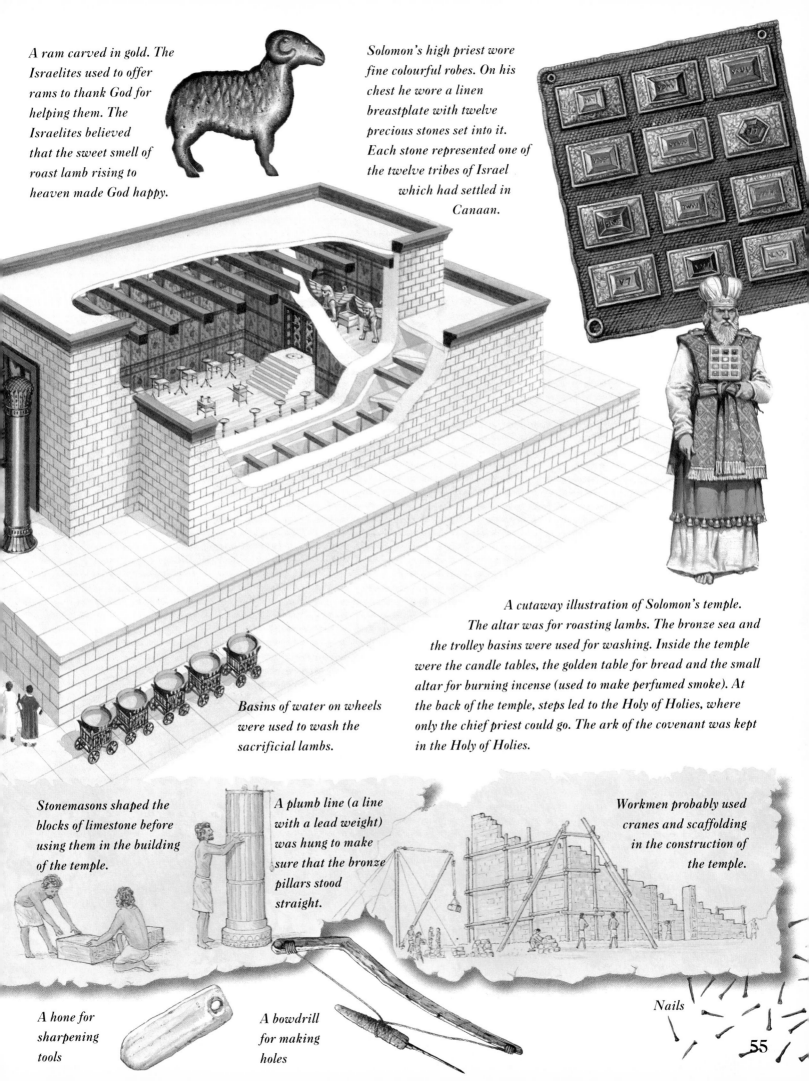

Basins of water on wheels were used to wash the sacrificial lambs.

A cutaway illustration of Solomon's temple. The altar was for roasting lambs. The bronze sea and the trolley basins were used for washing. Inside the temple were the candle tables, the golden table for bread and the small altar for burning incense (used to make perfumed smoke). At the back of the temple, steps led to the Holy of Holies, where only the chief priest could go. The ark of the covenant was kept in the Holy of Holies.

Stonemasons shaped the blocks of limestone before using them in the building of the temple.

A plumb line (a line with a lead weight) was hung to make sure that the bronze pillars stood straight.

Workmen probably used cranes and scaffolding in the construction of the temple.

A hone for sharpening tools

A bowdrill for making holes

Nails

55

The Visit of the Queen of Sheba

Solomon dreamed that God told him to make a wish and whatever it was it would be granted. Solomon replied, 'I am your servant and you have made me king in place of my father David. I am king over your chosen people, so give me the wisdom to rule your people and know the difference between right and wrong.' God was pleased with Solomon and replied, 'Because you have asked for this, and nothing for yourself, I will make you wise and also give you wealth and a long life.'

One day two women came to see King Solomon to ask him to settle their argument. One of the women explained the problem to the king: 'This woman and I live in the same house. I had a baby boy, then

Solomon imported purple-dyed cloth from Phoenicia. The Phoenicians lived along the coast and obtained the purple dye from a special sea-snail, called a murex.

A murex shell

three days later she had a baby boy. During the night this woman's son died because she lay on him. So she got up in the middle of the night and took my son while I was asleep. She put him in bed with her and put her dead baby in my bed. The next morning I found my son was dead! Then when I looked more closely I realized he was not my son at all.' The second woman said, 'No! The living one is my son. Yours is dead.' Solomon asked for a sword and said, 'Cut the living child in two and give one half to this woman and the other half to that woman.' The first

Egyptian jewellery, such as this necklace (left), and Phoenician glass vessels (right) were prized objects. They are the sort of trade goods that Solomon would have bought.

Solomon's merchant ships traded with countries in Asia and Africa. The king had a special interest in exotic animals and plants from faraway countries. From Asia he brought peacocks, apes and baboons. He also collected many different plants to use as spices and perfumes.

A patas monkey

A peacock

Spikenard, a spice used to perfume oils

woman was filled with horror and cried, 'Please give her the child. Don't kill him!' But the other woman said, 'Neither I nor you shall have him. Cut him in two.' Then Solomon said: 'Give the living baby to the first woman. Do not kill him. She is his mother.'

News of Solomon's wisdom soon spread far and wide. A very powerful queen from Sheba in the south of Arabia heard of Solomon's fame. She decided to travel to Jerusalem to meet him. She arrived with hundreds of camels carrying spices, gold and precious stones. She talked with Solomon and he was able to answer all her questions.

Solomon had never before met anyone as beautiful as the Queen of Sheba. They spent some time together, and then she returned home to her own country.

Solomon's empire (bordered by the red line) stretched from the River Euphrates in the north to the Red Sea. The empire later split into two kingdoms which were called Israel and Judah.

A camel caravan

THE TIME OF THE PROPHETS

Ivory comb

Ivory bedhead

Stories foreshadowing a nation's fall

Jezebel and the Palace of Ivory

When King Solomon died, the empire of the Israelites became weak. Solomon and David had both come from the kingdom of Judah in the south. The people of Judah expected that their future king would also come from Judah. But the people in Israel, the northern kingdom of the empire, wanted to have their own king.

The people of Israel rebelled and set up a capital at Samaria to rival Jerusalem in Judah. Samaria grew to be a prosperous city. One king of Israel, Ahab, was married to the Phoenician princess Jezebel. The Phoenicians were a sea-faring people, known for their skill at ivory

An ivory plaque of a sphinx carved by Phoenician craftsmen. A sphinx was a mythical creature with the head of a man, the body of a lion and hawk's wings.

Asherah

Astarte

Rashef

A bronze statue of Baal, the chief of the Canaanite gods. He was also worshiped by the Phoenicians. People believed that Baal could command the thunder and lightning.

El

These figures (left), known as idols, represent the gods of other religions practised at this time. The Israelites copied many of the customs of their neighbours and some followed their religions too.

carving. Ahab built a palace decorated with ivory for his wife. Ivory was a luxury, and the people of Israel were taxed in order to pay for Jezebel's palace. The Phoenician craftsmen who built the palace grew rich, while the people of Israel became poorer. The prophets thought that the ivory palace was an example of Ahab's and Jezebel's selfish and extravagant behaviour.

Jezebel was a powerful queen. When she married Ahab, she continued to worship Phoenician gods, particularly Baal. She built altars to these gods where the people of Israel came to worship.

The priests of Judah became worried that the people of Israel were no longer worshipping the real God who had led them out of Egypt and given them their laws. So Elijah, the most forceful and fiery of the prophets, issued a challenge to Baal.

Two wooden altars were set up, one for Baal, and one for God. The followers of Baal prayed to their god to set fire to his altar—but nothing happened. Elijah was so confident in his faith that he poured water over his altar three times, then prayed to God. The altar instantly burst into flames.

This ivory carving comes from Nimrud in Assyria. It shows a woman at a window wearing an Egyptian wig. Fragments of ivory with this same design were found at Jezebel's palace.

Jonah and the Great Fish

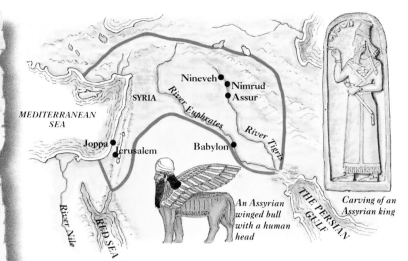

A map of the Assyrian Empire (bordered by the red line). The empire dominated the Near East from about 900 to 600 B.C.

Carving of an Assyrian king

An Assyrian winged bull with a human head

A powerful new kingdom, Assyria, arose in the east. The Assyrians showed their battle victories in wall carvings in their palaces. Visitors to their cities, including the capital at Nineveh, saw these pictures of prisoners hanging from poles or impaled on stakes. When they returned home they told stories of the cruel Assyrians.

These tales reached the prophet Jonah in Israel. God told Jonah, 'Go at once to the great city of Nineveh and speak out against it. I have heard of its wickedness.' Jonah was terrified by God's command and fled to the port of Joppa on the Mediterranean coast where he boarded a ship, hoping to escape from God.

Soon after the boat set sail, a storm blew up and the crew thought it would be wrecked. In a panic they threw the cargo overboard to lighten the ship, but it was no use. They prayed to their gods for help, but the storm still raged on. They decided to draw lots to find out whose wicked deed caused the gods' anger and this storm. The lot fell on Jonah. He told them he was running away from God, so the storm was his fault. 'Throw me overboard and the sea will become calm,' he said. The men felt

The inside of an Assyrian palace at Nimrud on the River Tigris. The walls were decorated with pictures of foreign kings and nobles paying taxes to the Assyrians. Huge statues of winged lions with human heads, stood proudly in the hall of the palace.

This Assyrian wall carving shows prisoners being led away, possibly to be tortured. Assyrian kings had conquered peoples transported to different parts of their empire to work as slaves.

Jonah was angry when God did not destroy Nineveh. 'Why was I put through all this?' Jonah thought. He sat outside the city and waited.

God made a vine grow over his head for shade, but the next day a worm chewed the vine and it withered. Jonah complained to God, and God replied, 'You are concerned about this vine, yet you did not tend it or make it grow. Nineveh has more than a hundred and twenty thousand people who cannot tell the difference between right and wrong. Should I not be concerned about them?' And so God showed mercy to the people of Nineveh because they repented.

sorry for Jonah and tried to row back to land, but the sea grew wilder. In the end they threw Jonah overboard, and the wind and rain stopped instantly. As Jonah sank into the sea, he was swallowed by a great fish. He stayed in its stomach for three days and nights, praying to God for forgiveness. After three days the fish vomited Jonah on to dry land, where he lay exhausted and fell asleep.

God spoke to Jonah again: 'Go to the wicked city of Nineveh.' Jonah awoke and was happy now to obey God. He went through the streets of Nineveh shouting, 'Forty more days and Nineveh will be destroyed.' To his surprise, the Assyrians believed him. The king took off his robes and covered himself with sackcloth. He knelt down in the dust and prayed to God for forgiveness. The people prayed, too, and fasted for forty days.

A reconstruction of the Assyrians capturing the city of Lachish near Jerusalem (see page 65). The powerful Assyrian army included archers and men with slings and spears. Battering rams were used to try to knock down the city walls.

The Fall of Israel

When Assyrian rulers conquered other countries, they stole their treasures and forced the people to pay taxes. In the middle of the ninth century B.C., twelve kings of conquered countries, including Ahab of Israel, united to fight against the powerful Assyrian Empire. But they were defeated and had to pay taxes to the emperor. Still, most of these smaller countries were left alone by the Assyrians and allowed to keep their lands.

However, in 745 B.C. the Assyrian emperor Tiglath-pileser (known as Pul in the Bible) wanted more. When Tiglath-pileser conquered Syria he took complete control of its lands. Neighbouring rulers panicked. Israel lost the lands of Galilee and Gilead in the north to Assyria. When Shalmaneser came to the Assyrian throne, the new Israelite king, Hoshea, tried to persuade the Egyptians to join him in a rebellion against Assyria.

The Egyptians were not interested, nor were any

MAKING A WOOLLEN GARMENT
The shearer cut wool from the coats of his sheep. The wool was then washed and dyed.

Shearing scissors

The wool was straightened with a metal comb

HOUSEHOLD ITEMS

An oil lamp

A stone flour mill

of Israel's old allies. Israel found itself alone. Hoshea was captured, and Israel gave up its lands until only the capital, Samaria, remained. The city held out for nearly two years before it surrendered.

Shalmaneser died at about this time, and the new emperor, Sargon, took more than twenty-seven thousand Israelites prisoner. The Assyrians made Samaria part of their empire and people from Syria, Babylon and Arabia came to live there. The Israelites who went into Assyria disappeared from history, and are known as the ten lost tribes of Israel.

A reconstruction of an Israelite home from the northern kingdom of Israel just before the Assyrian invasion. The walls were made of stone and covered with mud-plaster. The entrance led to a courtyard which was used as an open-air kitchen. Living rooms and rooms for cattle opened off the courtyard. At the back of the house was another large living room with a ladder leading up to sleeping quarters. A second ladder led to the roof, where grain and oil were stored in large jars.

Threads of wool were fed on to a spindle and spun into balls of yarn.

Most houses would have had a loom like this one to weave the yarn into rugs or clothing.

A bread oven

A strainer

A bronze whisk

63

Hezekiah's Troubles

A simple sundial made by placing a stick in the ground

An Egyptian sundial.

When Hezekiah became very ill he prayed to God. The shadow on the palace sundial moved backward as a sign from God that he would live for another fifteen years. Sundials use the shadow cast by the sun to tell the time.

Isaiah was a priest in the Temple of Jerusalem and one of the greatest prophets who ever lived. He was married to a prophetess and had two sons. Because of his special relationship with God, he could see into the future and advised the kings of Judah what to do.

Isaiah warned King Ahaz of Judah that what had just happened to Israel could also happen to Judah. He said that although Ahaz paid taxes to the Assyrians, the mighty empire of Assyria could cut down Judah as easily as a razor cuts through a beard.

But Ahaz wouldn't listen, nor would he stop worshipping pagan gods.

When Ahaz's son Hezekiah came to the throne of Judah, at the age of twenty-five, Isaiah told him to follow the true religion of his kingdom. Hezekiah obeyed him, destroying the pagan temples in Judah and inviting the citizens of Judah and conquered Israel to come to Jerusalem to celebrate the Passover feast. He did this because he thought that God would save the kingdom of Judah from the Assyrians.

But it was too late.

Pool of Siloam

Shaft leading inside the city

King Sennacherib of Assyria and his army began to move quickly from the north, conquering one city after another. They captured the city of Lachish, only fifty kilometres from Jerusalem.

King Hezekiah was so worried about Sennacherib's invasion that he developed a terrible boil. At this time most illness was thought to be brought on by a sin, and the only cure was to stop sinning. However, Isaiah ordered hot figs on a cloth to be laid on the boil. This was done and Hezekiah instantly recovered.

Hezekiah began to panic at the advance of the Assyrians. Against Isaiah's advice he asked the Egyptians for help in defeating the Assyrian army. But the Egyptians did not come to his aid.

Remembering how the people of

An Assyrian king on a hunting expedition. The king is about to throw his spear while a charioteer controls the horses and a servant stands by with more weapons. Lion hunting was a favourite sport of Assyrian kings.

Samaria had died of hunger and thirst, Hezekiah decided to build an underground tunnel to give the people of Jerusalem a water supply within the city walls. The tunnel would carry water from the Spring of Gihon outside the gates of Jerusalem to the Pool of Siloam inside the walls. The tunnel diggers managed to carve more than 500 metres through the earth with very simple tools.

Meanwhile, the Assyrians threatened to destroy Jerusalem if Hezekiah did not surrender. Isaiah assured him that God would not let Jerusalem fall to the Assyrians. Then strangely, overnight, a hundred and eighty-five thousand of the Assyrian soldiers who were camped near by suddenly died. Though Hezekiah was forced to continue paying Assyrian taxes, Jerusalem was saved.

Spring of Gihon

Hezekiah's tunnel diverted fresh water for fifty metres underneath the city. Two sets of diggers tunnelled towards each other from opposite ends. The men called out to each other as they dug so that their two short tunnels would meet to form one long tunnel.

The Burning of Jerusalem

Over a hundred years after the Assyrians destroyed Samaria, a new empire called Babylon arose east of the River Euphrates. With Babylon in the east and Egypt in the west, Judah had to side with one of these empires for protection.

Seeing the might of Babylon, Judah first befriended the Babylonians, but was then invaded by Neco of Egypt and had to make friends with the Egyptians instead. This enraged Nebuchadnezzar, the king of Babylon, and he ordered an invasion of Judah. When the king of Judah surrendered, Nebuchadnezzar made Zedekiah the new king.

The prophet Jeremiah warned Zedekiah not to rebel against Babylon, for he could not expect help from Egypt. The king's only hope was to trust God. But Zedekiah would not listen. When Nebuchadnezzar heard that Zedekiah planned to betray him, he ordered his army to attack Jerusalem. The people of Jerusalem believed that God would protect his city, but Jeremiah said the Israelites no longer deserved God's protection.

Jeremiah was thrown into prison and the people of Jerusalem

WEAPONS OF SIEGE WARFARE

A siege engine with battering ram

The battering ram was a long iron or wooden pole suspended from a rope. It was swung into the city's walls by soldiers who were inside the siege engine.

A pointed ram for pushing into cracks in the wall

A blunt ram for breaking sections of the wall

BABYLONIAN WEAPONS

A bronze axe head

A bow and quiver

prepared for the siege. After a year and a half the food ran out. Zedekiah was captured and the Babylonians burned Jerusalem to the ground. Nearly all the people of Judah were taken to Babylon as prisoners.

An attacking army would surround the city and try to cut off the water and food supply in order to starve the people into surrender. Then they tried to get through the city walls either by tunnelling under them or, if they were made of wood, by setting them alight . They would also set light to the wooden city gates. Ramps of stones, logs and trodden-down earth would be made to get over the walls. The tops of the walls were usually weaker, and easier to break.

Defenders threw flaming torches from the top of the walls to try and set the wooden battering rams alight.

Some attackers had long, arching shields to protect their heads from arrows. Others would put ladders up against the walls and try to climb over them.

A shield

A mace, a heavy club

THE EXILE

Plants from the gardens of Babylon

Stories of the exile to foreign lands and the rebirth of a nation

Life in Babylon

Some people, including Jeremiah, fled from Judah and found their way to Egypt, but about twenty thousand men, women and children were taken captive. King Nebuchadnezzar forced his prisoners to walk over a thousand kilometres to Babylon on the River Euphrates.

Babylon was well known as one of the most beautiful cities in the ancient world. The first thing the tired and hungry people of Judah saw when they arrived was a huge, magnificent blue gateway decorated with bulls and dragons. Inside the gates were 'hanging gardens' of exotic trees and splendid palaces. Although Babylonian kings and soldiers had a reputation for being cruel, the ordinary inhabitants of Babylon welcomed the people of Judah and treated them well. They settled in an area south of the main city of Babylon, called Nippur, and here they followed the advice Jeremiah had sent to captives in Babylon before Jerusalem's destruction: 'Build houses and live in them, plant gardens and eat their fruit, marry and have sons and daughters'.

Most of them took up the work they had done in Judah, such as farming and carpentry. Others became shopkeepers for the first time, buying and selling goods. Babylon was a busy city, ten times the size of Jerusalem. On the streets and squares, between massive temples to strange gods, life was noisy and colourful. Camel caravans, donkeys pulling carts, priests, pilgrims and traders flooded down the main streets. The temple authorities in Babylon ran their own shops, and banks fixed the prices of goods sold along the River Euphrates.

A broad, paved road led up to the main entrance of Babylon, the Ishtar gate. Bulls and dragons made of bricks decorated the high walls on either side. During festivals, great processions of people passed through the gateway carrying statues of their gods.

The Hanging Gardens of Babylon were one of the seven wonders of the ancient world. Nebuchadnezzar planted terraces of trees in the high courtyards of his palaces. One story says that he created the gardens for a foreign princess to remind her of her homeland.

Psalms and Music

For hundreds of years, from before the time of King David until after the Exile, the Hebrew people wrote and sang poems to tell of great disasters and celebrate times of joy. These musical poems are called psalms and were sung at festivals and on special occasions to glorify God and to remind the Israelites (or Jews as they became known) of their history. Much of Israel's great poetry can be found in the psalms. King David organized the Levite singers and wrote seventy-three of the psalms. While there was

A fragment of the Dead Sea scrolls, which were found in a cave at Qumran near the Dead Sea in 1947 by a shepherd boy. The scrolls were hidden in jars (see page 7) and placed inside the cave. They are the oldest surviving copy of the Hebrew Bible, including the psalms.

Music was arranged for the choir and orchestra of Levite priests who sang and played in the Jerusalem Temple. The instruments the priests played included cymbals, lyres, harps and trumpets.

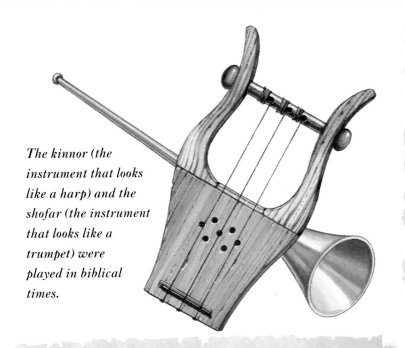

The kinnor (the instrument that looks like a harp) and the shofar (the instrument that looks like a trumpet) were played in biblical times.

much to celebrate in his day, many of the songs written during the Israelites' captivity in Babylon had sad themes:

By the rivers of Babylon we sat
    and wept
    when we remembered Zion.
        (Jerusalem)
There on the poplar trees
    we hung our harps,
    for there our captors asked us
    for songs.
[Psalm 137]

People sang when they wanted to thank God for helping them in times of need and they sang when they felt rejected and unable to understand God's ways:

We have heard with our ears,
    O God;
    our fathers have told us
what you did in their days,
    in days long ago.

With your hand you drove out
    the nations
    and planted our fathers...
Through you we push back our
    enemies;
    through your name we
    trample our foes...
But now you have rejected us;
    you no longer go out with
    our armies...
You gave us up to be
    devoured like sheep
    and have scattered us
    among the nations...
We are brought down to the dust;
    our bodies cling to the ground.
Awake, O God! Why do you sleep?
    Rouse yourself! Do not reject
    us for ever.
[Psalm 44]

In Psalm 44 the Israelites lament that they are defeated. The Israelites considered bowing a form of idol worship, and so a sin, but it was common practice for other biblical peoples. In this Egyptian relief, people bow down before an official.

71

Belshazzar's Feast

The empire of Babylon grew quickly under King Nebuchadnezzar. But the power became too much for him and he went mad. He became like a beast, sitting outside in the pouring rain eating grass.

Three kings came and went in the next seven years but none could rule the empire. But the Babylonians carried on as if nothing were wrong.

One such Babylonian was Prince Belshazzar. At a feast he held for a thousand guests, Belshazzar was drinking wine from the gold and silver goblets that Nebuchadnezzar had taken from the Temple at Jerusalem. Suddenly Belshazzar looked at one wall of his banqueting room in disbelief. A hand

without a body was writing a strange message on the wall: 'Mene, mene, tekel, u'pharsin'.

Belshazzar fell to the floor with fear. None of his wise men could understand the writing. The queen told him that a Jew named Daniel was at court and would be able to help. Daniel was summoned to reveal the meaning of the words:

Mene (measure): 'The days of your reign are numbered;

WEIGHTS AND MEASURES
Scales balanced precious stones against stones of a known weight.

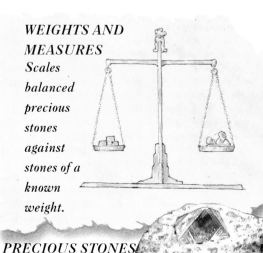

Bronze lion-weights like these from Assyria were used to value different amounts of goods. Weights came in the form of many living creatures including lions, ducks, frogs and insects.

PRECIOUS STONES AND METALS

Turquoise

Diamond

Lapis lazuli

God will bring your kingdom to an end.' Tekel (weight): 'You have been weighed and are found wanting.' U'pharsin (divide): 'Your kingdom will be divided and given to the Medes and the Persians.'

Belshazzar was grateful and rewarded Daniel, but the Medes (a powerful nation to the east) invaded Babylon and Belshazzar was killed.

The quay alongside the River Euphrates was outside the walls of Babylon. Ships loaded with gold, silver, spices and other precious goods arrived every day. Coins were not used to trade between different nations, so prices had to be agreed on in terms of a weight of gold or silver. On the wall at Belshazzar's feast were the words for the three weights: mene (mina), tekel (shekel) and u'pharsin (fraction). A mina was equal to sixty shekels. A fraction was a division of a weight.

Bath measures were used for measuring liquid goods such as wine and oil. There were different sizes for different amounts of liquid. The largest was the donkey-load or kor.

Solid goods such as cereals were measured in large containers. An ephah was large enough to hold a woman. An omer was a tenth of an ephah.

An ephah

An omer

Mother-of-pearl

Gold

Ruby

Silver

73

Queen Esther

It was soon the turn of the Persians to attack Babylon. They cleverly diverted the River Euphrates and marched into the city along its dry river bed. After Babylon was defeated, many Jews went to live in Susa, the capital of the Persian Empire, where they soon rose to high positions in the government and the army. It was a quiet time when Jews and other foreigners were free to live as they pleased. Greek doctors, Babylonian astronomers and Phoenician explorers all lived and worked together peacefully. When Xerxes (called Ahasuerus in the Bible) was emperor of Persia, a

A gold bracelet belonging to a Persian queen. Gold captured from the enemies of the Persians was melted down and made into new jewellery by Persian craftsmen.

A Persian guard. The Persian king had a royal bodyguard of a thousand bowmen. These bowmen were called 'The Immortals' (people who never die) because whenever one of them fell in battle there was always another one to replace him. This guard is wearing a rope headband, leather boots and fine clothes. His long spear is tipped with silver.

beauty contest was held to find him a new queen. He chose Esther, an orphan who had been brought up by her cousin Mordecai. An official named Haman hated the Jews and Mordecai, and plotted to kill them. He persuaded Xerxes, who did not know that Esther was a Jew, that the Jews were dangerous. By drawing lots, Xerxes decided that on the thirteenth day of that month all Jews would be killed.

Mordecai asked Esther to try to persuade the king not to allow this terrible thing. But Esther was scared, for she knew that by law anyone who approached the king unsummoned would be killed. Despite her fear, Esther approached Xerxes, but only to ask him and Haman to dinner. At this dinner, she asked them to

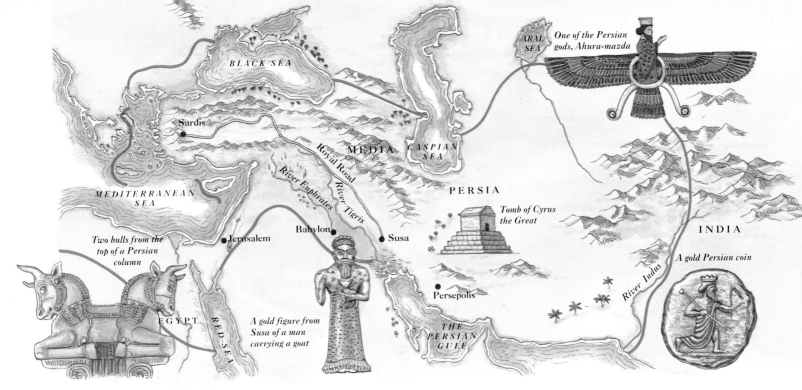

One of the Persian gods, Ahura-mazda

BLACK SEA

Sardis

MEDIA

CASPIAN SEA

ARAL SEA

MEDITERRANEAN SEA

Royal Road

River Euphrates

River Tigris

PERSIA

Tomb of Cyrus the Great

INDIA

Two bulls from the top of a Persian column

Jerusalem

Babylon

Susa

A gold Persian coin

River Indus

EGYPT

RED SEA

A gold figure from Susa of a man carrying a goat

Persepolis

THE PERSIAN GULF

The Persian Empire (bordered by the red line) was larger than the Assyrian and Babylonian empires. It stretched from India to Egypt. The Persian king appointed governors to control each province (area) in his empire.

another banquet the next day. That night Xerxes decided to honour Mordecai because he had once saved his life. But Haman thought the honour was to be his. When Xerxes asked Haman to dress Mordecai in fine robes and escort him on horseback through the city, Haman was disgraced.

At Esther's second

A carving of the Persian king Darius I, father of Xerxes. Darius was an excellent general who built roads, such as the Royal Road, all over his empire to ensure fast communication between himself and his subjects.

dinner, she told Xerxes of Haman's plot to kill the Jews—and that the Jews were her people. Xerxes stormed into the garden in a rage. Haman threw himself at Esther and begged for mercy. When Xerxes returned to see Haman sprawled over his queen, he could not control his anger and ordered him to be hanged.

By law, Xerxes could not withdraw his order to kill the Jews. But at Esther's request he allowed Jews to protect themselves. To celebrate the law, the Jews held a feast called Purim, named after 'Pur', the Hebrew word for 'lot', in memory of the lot drawn to decide the date for the execution of the Jews.

Silver and gold coins depicting kings of Persia.

The Return to Jerusalem

I n the first year of Persian rule over Babylon, Cyrus the Great allowed the exiled Jews to return home. Forty-two thousand people set off on the long journey to Jerusalem. Priests led the long caravan, while two hundred singers kept up the spirits of the men, women and children who followed slowly behind. Eventually the long-awaited day arrived. Amid the brown hills of Judah they saw the ruins of Jerusalem.

This clay barrel records some of the things Cyrus the Great did when he became king. It describes how he allowed Jewish temples to be rebuilt.

The new arrivals from Babylon started to rebuild the city and the Temple. But with no homes and very little to eat, people soon became more concerned with looking after themselves. They also had to face attacks from their northern neighbours, the Samaritans. These people were Jews who had not been taken into captivity when the Assyrians conquered Israel. They also felt the land belonged to them.

News of these troubles reached Nehemiah who was the cup-bearer to the Persian king. He persuaded the king to make him governor

An aerial view of the city of Jerusalem, showing the walls that Nehemiah built to keep the city's inhabitants safe from attack. The walls enclosed the old site of Solomon's Temple and David's city. The Temple was also rebuilt by Nehemiah and the returning exiles.

of Judah so that he could help to sort out their problems. He set off from Babylon with a team of builders to rebuild the city walls.

But defence of the city was not the only problem. The people of Jerusalem were not following the laws God gave to Moses. Many had forgotten their history and did not know the Hebrew language or the laws of Moses. They needed a leader like Moses to show them how to live as God wanted.

The man who did this was Ezra, a priest living in Persia. When he came to Jerusalem, all the city assembled in

After the time of Ezra scribes became important teachers of the law of Moses. Scribes also performed social functions such as recording business transactions and writing letters for people.

the Temple court. From dawn till noon, Ezra read out the law from his scroll. As he read, his scribes translated the scripture into Aramaic which everyone understood. They also explained the difficult parts of the law. The people listened carefully and realized how wrongly they were living. They felt ashamed and asked for forgiveness, But they were glad they had found out how to follow God again. All Jews in the ancient Near East now believed they were one people again because they all shared the law of Moses.

This is how a Jewish synagogue in Persia at about this time may have looked. Synagogues were places of worship. They were built by Jews who lived in foreign countries where there was no Temple of Jerusalem.

LONDON BOROUGH OF BARKING AND DAGENHAM SCHOOL LIBRARIES

Index